# IMMERSION

# IMMERSION

## THE SCIENCE OF THE EXTRAORDINARY AND THE SOURCE OF HAPPINESS

## PAUL J. ZAK

LIONCREST
PUBLISHING

IMMERSION

*The Science of the Extraordinary and the Source of Happiness*

FIRST EDITION

ISBN  978-1-5445-3197-7  *Hardcover*
      978-1-5445-3195-3  *Paperback*
      978-1-5445-3196-0  *Ebook*

*To Jorge Barraza and Scott Brown who have dedicated years of effort helping me bring Immersion to life.*

# CONTENTS

# INTRODUCTION

"I INTERROGATE TERRORISTS FOR A LIVING AND I NEED THAT STUFF TOMORROW!"

At 6'4", it is rare for me to be nose-to-nose with anyone, and Ron Wilson was not only my height but also had thirty pounds on me. And here he was, just inches from my face, vigorously throwing this line at me.

I had no way of knowing it at the time, but that growling statement was the start of my journey into the science of the extraordinary. The intelligence officer standing before me made it perfectly clear: the CIA needed to get information from terrorists subjected to extraordinary rendition about deadly attacks on US troops, and they needed it now. It would be my job to uncover methods that interrogators could use to persuade extradited terrorists to give up vital secrets.

Soon enough, I was presenting my findings at DARPA (the Defense Advanced Research Projects Agency), the US Department of Defense's research arm. I described how my lab had discovered that the neurochemical oxytocin is released in the brain when someone is shown trust by another person and how oxytocin motivates people to cooperate. If an interrogator could get a terrorist's brain to make oxytocin, I argued, there was a chance he would become cooperative. Wilson wanted a more immediate solution and suggested administering synthetic oxytocin to terrorists' brains. After all, we had done just that with healthy adults in some of our studies.

In the end, getting a terrorist to blurt out where Osama bin Laden was hiding would prove to be more complicated than good cop, bad cop or administering oxytocin. What this early research did provide, however, was the catalyst to figure out why humans crave extraordinary experiences.

Ten years later, I was sitting next to retired Lt. Col. William Casebeer, who was my program officer at DARPA, at Marine Corps Base Quantico. "General on deck!" the voice boomed from the front of the packed conference room as the entire assembly stood and saluted. I had been invited to a briefing on US assistance to one of the countries that had transitioned to a fragile democracy after the Arab Spring. US military advisors were being sent that evening to support the new government, and they wanted to know if the technology I had developed with DARPA support could be deployed to improve the government's communication with its citizens. The DARPA funding helped me identify neural signals that accurately predicted the actions people would take after a message or experience. At the time of the Quantico briefing, special forces soldiers had started using software based on my research to create communications that would motivate cooperation with US forces.

To my knowledge, the US government has never used my research findings during interrogations or "kinetic" operations. With just a few exceptions, combat operations and claustrophobic interrogation rooms are venues that inhibit the neural conditions of influence.

## NEUROSCIENCE IN ACTION

For over two decades, I have been on a quest to understand human social behaviors. What makes us happy? Why do some teams work together more effectively than others? Why are some experiences transformative? These are a few of the questions I've investigated in my work as a behavioral neuroscientist. This research has taken me from the Pentagon to Fortune 50 boardrooms to the rainforest of Papua New Guinea in order to measure brain activity as people do what people do, all to understand and predict how people will behave. And what causes these behaviors. While clandestine agencies of the US government funded my early research, ultimately I discovered how to create extraordinary experiences.

The first step in engineering an amazing experience is to identify how the brain differentiates between extraordinary and ordinary. As I will explain in Chapter 1, when the extraordinary occurs, a particular and peculiar set of brain signals I have named "Immersion" appear. When the brain is immersed in an experience, something extraordinary happens. Not only do people enjoy immersive experiences, but they also remember them, share them, and they influence behavior.

In the past ten years, I've helped businesses, governments, and individuals create extraordinary experiences that bring happiness to customers, employees, and audiences. I've even helped couples find love on TV. The software platform my colleagues and I built from this research is currently being used by hundreds of organizations to radically improve marketing, sales, entertainment, customer experiences, and corporate training. Knowing what is highly valued by the brain enables businesses to avoid offering customers the bleak, monotonous, and uninteresting.

More than avoiding the ordinary, extraordinary experiences create a craving to repeat the experience. As a result, businesses that consistently provide the extraordinary to their customers are extraordinarily profitable. But there is an even bigger takeaway. The approach I describe in this book will enable you to curate your life for greater happiness. Extraordinary experiences are peak moments that add to the quality of life.

## THE MONOTONY OF THE MUNDANE

So, why doesn't every organization and every person tap into the power of Immersion? As we will see, creating extraordinary experiences is extraordinarily hard without the right guidance. Most of our lives are filled with the mundane.

For example, every day 24,000 new songs are released worldwide—that's 168,000 new songs every week. Ninety-five percent of them are streamed ten times or less (that's the band and their moms). In 2019, Hollywood released 786 movies; only 20% of them earned a profit. The same is true year after year. And it continues: 65% of TV shows are canceled after their first season, and 15% of video games generate 90% of the profits earned by gaming companies. Most creative content is simply not good enough to gain an audience.

Monotony permeates education as well. Students struggle to pay attention for six or seven hours, let alone learn something. This occurs, in part, because teachers are rarely equipped with the resources and knowledge to effectively engage and inspire students. So mind-numbing monotony becomes the norm.

Consider the plethora of misguided, tone-deaf, and ineffective advertising. The number of fails is staggering, from the Kendall Jenner Pepsi commercial that tried to hijack the Black Lives Matter movement, to the Hyundai ad that trivialized suicide, to the Bud Light spot with the tagline "The perfect beer for removing *no* from your vocabulary for the night."

The mistakes keep coming: professional presentations that put their audiences to sleep, call center associates who incite rage, supervisors who are unable to lead employees to anything close to excellence, and politicians who bluster without connecting to voters. Mundane experiences waste time and money, frustrate customers, and damage reputations. In a nutshell, the mundane makes people unhappy.

Movie studios, TV executives, music producers, advertising agencies, and retailers are all under enormous pressure to create amazing experiences. They hire "artists" to somehow create hits.

Except they often don't.

The best of these artists only produce winners 30% of the time.

The reason for all of the failures? Creators of experiences use intuition to determine what people will love. "Intuition" is a polite way of saying they are guessing. These guesses may be informed by training and experience, but they are still guesses. After winning an Academy Award for directing *Scent of a Woman*, Martin Brest wrote and directed Ben Affleck and Jennifer Lopez in *Gigli*, which is considered one of the worst movies ever made. He never worked again. Even the great Steven Spielberg helmed 2016's *The BFG* to a $100 million loss.

Some experience creators use feedback to try to improve their content. Traditionally, they ask people to rate how much they "like" something. Guess what? People lie. Not maliciously—most of us simply want to avoid the awkwardness of saying we dislike something. Similarly, when market researchers ask people to report what they "like" in surveys, the answers are nearly always worthless. If "liking" something meant people would love it, the failure rates of all kinds of experiences would not be so high.

Steve Jobs said, "People don't know what they want until you show it to them. That's why I never rely on market research. Our task is to read things that are not yet on the page." Neuroscience techniques are now able to do exactly this: measure the value someone actually gets from an experience. Measuring people's unconscious neurologic responses enables content creators to consistently produce hits. Even better, recent technological advances allow anyone to measure neurologic value in real time without the need for scientific training.

In Greek mythology, king Sisyphus was punished by the gods and forced to roll a boulder up a hill, only to have it roll back down, for eternity. What Sisyphus was missing was a tool to keep the rock from rolling. Marketers, experience designers, educators, and film executives are also missing a tool—something to ensure that the content they create is spectacular. More often than not, enormous effort is put into creating content that rolls to the bottom of the hill. Here's the good news: we now have the ability to solve this problem, and it is based on recently developed science.

## UNDERSTANDING THE WHY BEHIND THE EXTRAORDINARY

After measuring neurologic Immersion in more than fifty thousand people, I have been able to reverse engineer the process of creating the extraordinary. This approach—measuring brain activity in a moderate number of people to forecast outcomes—is known as "brain as predictor." Brain activity predicts, with 83–97% accuracy, which movies and TV shows will be hits, why some stores handily outsell others, and which learners will remember the details of training weeks later.

Most importantly, the science identifies the why, not just the what. As pioneering computer scientist and Rear Admiral Grace Hopper said, "One accurate measurement is worth a thousand expert opinions." When you know why an experience is extraordinary, then you can apply the principles outlined in this book to nearly any situation.

The examples in the book show you how others have created extraordinary experiences as a guide to doing this yourself. They come from two decades of neuroscience experiments in my academic laboratory and use of the Immersion software platform I created, which is used by businesses worldwide. The platform democratized neuroscience, allowing anyone, anywhere, to measure what brains love. Watching the data live while people have an experience is like putting a speedometer on people's brains. The platform shows Immersion second-by-second for activities as varied as children absorbing a math lesson in a fourth-grade classroom, people watching TED Talks, team meetings at the largest tech companies, and executives choosing a trailer for the next $100 million movie. No matter the setting, the data show experience designers how to improve the impact of their experiences by 10x.

Without the science, the examples in this book would be based on experiences that were deemed extraordinary after the fact. But there's a problem with explaining the extraordinary through this lens. Our self-aggrandizing recall of events ensures that we knew Adele's "Easy on Me" would break the record for most Spotify streams in a single day (over twenty-four million) or that *My Big Fat Greek Wedding* would earn its producers a 7,000% return on their investment. The retrospective is fraught with hindsight bias, but this is extinguished by prospective data.

The world is rapidly transforming into the "experience economy." Once our basic needs are met, we increasingly crave extraordinary experiences. A study from Harvard University reported that people spend up to 40% of conversations informing others about their experiences. As the planet gets richer, people are less interested in getting stuff and more interested in doing stuff—and then telling their friends about it. This is especially true for millennials and younger generations. As a result, the ability to identify and consistently create extraordinary experiences is absolutely essential.

Many businesses understand the importance of extraordinary experiences. Brands like Sephora, the Disney Store, and American Girl stores are destination retailers in which the shopping experience is as important as the purchases. At IPIC Theaters, waiters serve upscale food and drinks during movies. At SafeHouse restaurant in Milwaukee, patrons use a password to enter as spies on a mission. Starbucks founder Howard Schultz understood that a café offered an experience, not just coffee. His company recently upped their game with Starbucks Reserve Roasteries, which takes the café experience to a new level. Patrons watch green coffee beans being roasted and then brewed on-site, while "mixologists" host coffee tastings and prepare unique cocktails. People can even shop for local artwork and gifts with drinks in hand.

Extraordinary experiences are not always upmarket; great experiences are filtering into down-market businesses too. Low-cost airline Avelo flies only to and from regional airports that are easy to navigate. The airline incentivizes checked bags in order to speed up boarding and deplaning and does not charge flight-change fees. Budget-conscious passengers are able to enjoy an experience they typically don't get, one that is both easy and comfortable.

Businesses have learned that extraordinary experiences build brand attachment and customer loyalty. While one negative experience can drive away a customer for life, one fantastic experience can cause a customer to buy again and again. The data show that the same attachment to extraordinary content benefits advertisers, producers of entertainment, educators, and corporate trainers. Extraordinary experiences move people to take action and enjoy the process.

In each chapter, I will draw insights from experience designers who have profoundly improved the impact of their work by measuring Immersion. These insights reveal the steps you can take to create extraordinary experiences without having to measure neural responses. Along the way, you will learn a bit more neuroscience in the service of a clear understanding of how to create the extraordinary. The key takeaways are summarized at the end of each chapter, giving you a framework to improve the type of experience the chapter has focused on. The final chapter shows how immersive experiences increase people's happiness and makes the case that content and experience creators are improving people's lives by giving them moments of joy.

We want extraordinary, not ordinary. We will wait in line for extraordinary, pay more for extraordinary, and post about extraordinary on social media. Soon you'll know how to create the extraordinary too.

But first, we need to learn just a little about the brain.

# CHAPTER 1

# THE SCIENCE OF IMMERSION

Nine months after its release, I rewatched the Academy Award–winning movie *La La Land*. I had seen the film in a theater and enjoyed it immensely, shedding tears during the powerful ending. My second viewing was at home by myself, and I cried at the ending again, even though I knew what would happen. But why would the second showing still be so powerful? The story is rich in emotional nuance, and when watching it again, I was surprised by parts of the movie I had missed during the first showing when I was focused on the storyline. I enjoyed the movie in a different way by absorbing the story's subtleties. Extraordinary experiences generate powerful emotional responses. This is why we remember them so well. But it is also why they are so hard to describe.

How good was *La La Land* for me? I really like the movie, maybe a nine or even a ten out of ten. My daughter, who watched *La La Land* with me in the theater, gave it an eight out of ten. Here's the problem: what does an "eight" or "nine" mean? What are these values based on or compared to? We could average these "liking" scores across a bunch of people and then, maybe, have some idea about the quality of *La La Land*. But, without having an objective anchor for "liking," averaging people's responses has little meaning. We know this because "liking" ratings have almost no predictive value for movie ticket sales or Academy Awards or other performance measures. The subjective poorly predicts the objective.

As social creatures, people try to fit in by saying the "right" thing. This causes another problem. If a market researcher asks, "Wasn't that movie great? How would you rate it from one to ten?" people will report higher "liking" values. We are primed by the statement that the movie was great and therefore rate the experience as better than we might do so otherwise. These priming effects can be very subtle; even a questioner's smile can make a difference. As I discuss in Chapter 2, advertisers use priming all the time to influence behavior.

A clever experiment in 1974 demonstrated the fragility of self-reported data. Researchers from the University of British Columbia and the State University of New York in Stony Brook asked heterosexual male participants to report their attraction to a female research assistant. In the control condition, the men completed a questionnaire after crossing a sturdy bridge a few feet over a small stream. Like most young straight guys would, they reported moderately high attraction to the research assistant. In the treatment condition, the attraction question was asked after participants crossed a suspension bridge high above a deep ravine. Walking across a soaring bridge increases physiologic arousal—resulting in a pounding heart and sweaty palms. When participants in this condition were asked to report their attraction to the research assistant, they said they were very interested in dating her. Why?

There is bidirectional feedback from body to brain and back again. We rationalize our physiologic states to reflect a presumed emotional state. In the bridge experiment, the participants' brains unconsciously processed increased arousal, and the conscious part of their brains rationalized a reason for this: strong attraction to the research assistant. The clever design of this experiment hid the bridge in plain sight so participants did not associate their arousal with being suspended far above the earth. This is known as the "misattribution of arousal," and studies show we fall prey to it all the time. So, if one is highly aroused—or, for that matter, under-aroused—after an experience and asked to explain this, their conscious brain will rationalize an answer that may have nothing to do with the physiologic response.

I'll put a finer point on this. Some of my experiments measure neurophysiologic responses in animals. The BBC asked me to design an experiment to measure the neurobiology of cross-species animal "friendships." They flew me to Arkansas where I drove to an animal refuge in the Ozark mountains. I would be taking blood samples, so I needed dry ice to freeze the plasma I would extract. Before filming, I loaded fifty pounds of dry ice into a disposable ice chest I'd bought at Walmart and put it in the trunk of my rented car. Many of my experiments involve blood draws, so driving with dry ice is something I do regularly. At some point during the one-hour drive to the animal refuge, I started breathing heavily. My conscious response was,

"I am really excited about being on this show." Then I started panting like a dog and realized that something was wrong. I pulled over, got out of the car and took a few deep breaths of fresh Arkansas oxygen. The carbon dioxide from the dry ice had been leaking into the car's passenger compartment. My brain stem signaled that I needed more oxygen and increased my respiration rate to compensate. When this effect started, though, I rationalized my fast breathing as excitement.

Another reason to suspect that "liking" ratings are bogus is that our brains chunk experiences to ease recall. We tend to remember the emotional peaks of experiences and whatever happened at the end. This is especially true for longer experiences. Psychologists have named this the "peak-end rule." If *La La Land* were a so-so movie but ended with a highly emotional scene, when asked to report how good it was, most people would give it a high rating. The structure of an experience affects how we recall it, something we'll delve into when we discuss how advertisers link emotional responses to brands in the next chapter.

A final issue that arises when asking people how much they like something is that the measurement instrument, the body, is buffeted by internal and external factors that affect ratings. If you are hungry, or distracted, have to pee, or are sitting next to a gorgeous guy or girl, copious research shows that your ratings will change. This is another reason why people lie in surveys. Survey takers try to balance out these effects by asking questions to a large number of people, but "liking" answers are generally all over the map, so the average is still not very meaningful. People in the know know this. English filmmaker Ridley Scott, famous for directing hits like *Alien*,

*The Martian,* and *Gladiator,* has said he ignores test screening responses because randomly chosen audiences are not storytellers and seldom understand the nuances of moviemaking. Test audiences disliked many films that became classics, including Martin Scorsese's *Cape Fear,* Francis Ford Coppola's *Apocalypse Now,* and key parts of the 1939 classic *The Wizard of Oz.* John Frankenheimer, respected director of *The Birdman of Alcatraz* and *The Manchurian Candidate* said, "You spend a year making a movie, then it comes down to twenty morons in a focus group. They all want to be film critics and are given a chance suddenly." Yet movie studios are more confident in their decisions when they have data, even if the data are worthless.

How about a different approach to "liking." Pollsters since the 1980s have asked audiences to turn dials while an experience is happening to report whether it is dull or divine. My group's studies have found that dial turns poorly predict objective outcomes like purchases or TV ratings. The purportedly scientific technique of turning a dial faces the same problem we discussed earlier: it asks people to consciously report their unconscious emotional reactions. This just can't be done with veracity. Dial turns also induce a second problem: one is necessarily taken out of the experience in order to turn a dial to rate it.

To consistently create extraordinary experiences, one must have a measurement technology that objectively measures the specific emotional responses associated with those experiences. But what exactly are those emotions?

## EXTRAORDINARY EMOTIONS

I vividly recall when my future wife boarded an airplane I was on in Cincinnati, Ohio, and sat in front of me. I remember exactly what she was wearing and how she looked. What I cannot tell you is why I decided to tap her on the shoulder and start talking to her. And she cannot tell you why she invited me to sit in the empty seat next to her. "Something" seemed to be happening, although neither of us can describe it. But it was extraordinary.

Extraordinary experiences are often described as "mind-blowing." Think how easy it is to recall when you met your romantic partner. Or the concert you attended where the band performed an unannounced duet with a famous rock star. Or when you were unexpectedly upgraded to first class (perhaps when you and your daughter were flying home from Hawaii—thank you United Airlines).

Extraordinary experiences have the following qualities: *they are unexpected, emotionally charged, narrow one's focus to the experience itself, are easy to remember,* and *provoke actions.* The components of the extraordinary come as a package, not in isolation from each other.

## MILLION-DOLLAR QUESTION

A couple of years ago, I was invited to a dinner in which the guest list was kept secret and we were asked to make up names for ourselves. The organizer, Jon Levy, who started a group called The Influencers, uses this subterfuge to keep the attendees—all experts in their chosen fields—from engaging in "shop talk." One of the dinner guests introduced himself as "Doc," but I knew right away that he was Adam Savage, the chattier half of the *MythBusters* duo. In fact, I had attended *MythBusters* Live with my daughter a few weeks before meeting Adam at dinner. As two of the older attendees, we stuck close together for the next several hours talking about the many odd scientific experiments we had both run. I told him I use the *MythBusters* credo in my lab: always start experiments at small scale. If that works, then scale up.

This is what I did when my lab started studying extraordinary experiences. Indeed, my motivation to understand such experiences was entirely personal.

I fly several times a month (right now I'm typing on a plane off the coast of Africa). I love to fly, love airplanes, and love adventures. Cross-country flights are a wonderful five-hour bubble to get work done without being disturbed. Some years ago I was flying home from Washington, DC, happily working away, when the plane hit constant turbulence. The skygods had decreed that I should stop working and watch a movie. Two hours later, I discovered that I am the last person you want to sit next to on an airplane.

I had decided to watch the movie *Million Dollar Baby*. I hadn't seen it, but I figured after a hard week I deserved to watch a Clint Eastwood-directed film that had won the Best Picture Academy Award. It is a wonderful movie, and I became deeply absorbed in it. The narrative is about two strangers who form a father-daughter relationship, and it concludes with an agonizing decision by Clint Eastwood's character. When the movie was over, the man next to me poked me in the shoulder and said, "Sir, do you need help?" I was crying.

Well, not really crying, more like heaving big sloppy sobs from my eyes, nose, and mouth. Everyone around could hear me, but I could not suppress my sadness. It was really weird and embarrassing!

After I recovered, I began to wonder what had happened to me. I was cognitively intact, aware of my surroundings and who I was. I hadn't had a drink or taken drugs, I hadn't had a stroke, and I was psychologically stable. And yet the story was so powerful that it caused my brain to react as if I were a character in the movie, as if one of my own daughters were suffering. I experienced deep heartache as the movie ended. But it was only a fictional story.

The movie must have changed my brain activity in some way, but how?

## NEUROSCIENCE PRINCIPLES

The brain is doing hundreds of things at once. So how can we have any confidence that measured brain activity causes a behavior? The short answer is by repeating experiments in different ways, on different people, and using different measurement instruments. It is important for you to get a sense of how we do this so you have confidence in the principles discussed in this book. So we need to spend a bit of time on the science.

The bugaboo in neuroscience is known as the "signal extraction" problem. Right now, the vast majority of your brain activity is devoted to keeping you upright, breathing, and conscious. Very small ribbons of neural activity are responding to the information in this book. Finding the ribbons of neural activity that correspond to an experience, and only to that experience, is like looking for a needle in an eighty-six-billion-neuron haystack.

My lab resolves the signal extraction problem through a cascade of techniques. First, when we investigate a new experience, we start by measuring changes in neurochemicals from baseline levels by taking blood samples. If we see neurochemical changes, we focus the next experiment's data collection on regions of the brain and body that are rich in receptors for these neurochemicals. Neuroscience instruments can measure electrical activity at up to one thousand times a second, providing a detailed map of how the brain is responding. Unlike many other groups, my lab measures neural responses multiple ways simultaneously to increase our confidence that we are finding the true activity associated with an experience and not the brain's background machinations. For example, we often run experiments in which we simultaneously measure the electrical activity of the brain using an electroencephalogram while also capturing the brain's control of the heart using an electrocardiogram. We might even capture the brain's arousal system by measuring the tiny changes in electrical activity due to sweat on the fingers and palms.

Next we use pharmaceuticals to safely trace out brain networks by tuning their volume up or down. Go figure: you can pay people to take drugs in experiments! In addition, all our experiments ask participants to do something. We can then relate changes in neurophysiology to actions in order to predict what people will do. The combination of multiple experiments and multiple measurements is used to identify if the experience was extraordinary.

A note about terminology: throughout this book I will use the following terms interchangeably: *neural, neurophysiologic, neurologic,* and *physiologic.* They all refer to activity of the nervous system, both the brain and the nerves outside the brain; while they have subtle differences in a technical sense, in casual use they mean the same thing.

## ENTER OXYTOCIN

After my breakdown watching *Million Dollar Baby,* I realized I had stumbled onto a potentially useful way to extend my studies of the social brain. My lab was the first to discover that the neurochemical oxytocin is released in the human brain when one is trusted, and that this molecule motivates the person who was trusted to reciprocate by being trustworthy. Since its discovery by Henry Dale in 1906, oxytocin has revealed itself to be an astonishingly interesting molecule. It is a small peptide synthesized in the hypothalamus of mammals' brains. Made of only nine amino acids, it is quite fragile. Oxytocin functions both as a hormone (binding to receptors on organs in the body) and as a neuromodulator (binding to receptors on neurons in the brain). Oxytocin is the quintessential mammalian peptide, being part of a cascade of factors facilitating live birth and care for offspring. Early studies focused on oxytocin's contraction of the uterus and its binding to receptors in the breast to initiate milk letdown. Animal studies have shown that during social interactions oxytocin is released simultaneously in the brain and body. This is unusual for a brain-derived neurochemical, and it provides a powerful way to study oxytocin: after a social encounter, changes in oxytocin in the blood reflect changes in oxytocin in the brain.

While interesting, oxytocin is a challenging molecule to measure. It has a three-minute half-life and weak chemical bonds. My research team discovered—by repeatedly poking me in the arm—that rapid blood draws could capture an oxytocin spike. But the tubes of blood have to be kept cold so the chemical bonds do not degrade. Immediately after the blood draw, the tubes are put into an ice bath and then centrifuged at just above freezing to keep the oxytocin intact. After centrifugation, the blood's plasma, where oxytocin is found, is extracted and then stored at minus seventy degrees centigrade in an ultracold freezer until we analyze it. Doing this properly requires the right equipment and a lot of practice.

Once we developed a way to measure the acute release of oxytocin in humans, my lab began running experiments measuring oxytocin during social interactions of nearly every type. These experiments were done in my laboratory as well as in field studies of religious rituals, folk dances, weddings, and even during a war dance by Indigenous people in the rainforest of Papua New Guinea. In all these experiments, when people socialized, oxytocin was produced and helping behaviors followed.

My research proved that oxytocin signals that a person appears safe to be around. Perhaps most surprising, in humans, this "you seem trustworthy" signal occurs between strangers and even happens without face-to-face interactions. We humans are acutely aware of behaviors that signal safety or hostility.

I also pioneered a way to safely inject synthetic oxytocin into human brains to prove that oxytocin directly causes prosocial behaviors. My technique sprays oxytocin into the sinuses and, in about forty-five minutes, enough crosses the blood-brain barrier to bathe the brain with oxytocin. I've done this hundreds of times without any adverse effects on participants. My lab's research, confirmed by others, has shown that oxytocin influences social behaviors by increasing empathy. When empathy is revved up, people nearly always treat others with care and kindness. The brain's oxytocin response follows from nearly any positive social interaction and persists in the brain for about thirty minutes.

The experience I had watching *Million Dollar Baby* caused me to wonder if movies, in addition to the personal interactions I had already studied, would cause the brain to make oxytocin. My colleague Jorge Barraza and I decided to run an experiment to measure the neurochemical response to short videos. We took blood samples before and immediately after people watched two versions of a video.

We started small-scale.

## BEN'S STORY

I wanted to replicate the response I'd had watching *Million Dollar Baby*, but without using a two-hour movie and an airplane. Jorge found a twelve-minute video from St. Jude Children's Research Hospital that we were given permission to use. We clipped out a one-hundred-second video of a father talking to the camera while his two-year-old son, Ben, who has terminal brain cancer, plays in the background. The story has a classic narrative arc in which the father struggles to connect to and enjoy his son, knowing that the child has only weeks to live. The clip concludes with the father finding the strength to stay emotionally close to his son "until he takes his last breath." The video is highly emotional—I showed it at a law conference and a number of hardened lawyers cried.

We thought the video's emotionality might provoke an oxytocin response. For comparison, we extracted another one-hundred-second clip showing the same father and son at the zoo. This version does not mention cancer or death, but one notices that the boy is bald and the voice-over calls him "miracle boy." This video lacks the narrative structure and emotionality of the first video; there is no crisis, no emotional turmoil, and no heroic decision. But it has the same characters and is the same length as the emotional video.

Neurochemicals are constantly changing, so we needed a way to determine if changes were the result of the video and not just due to housekeeping done by the brain. Since we were causing mild pain to participants by drawing their blood twice, we paid them forty dollars for their time and discomfort. After the second blood draw, participants were given an opportunity to donate some of their earnings to St. Jude's. We presumed that if they donated money, the stories must have "gotten to them," just like *Million Dollar Baby* had gotten to me. The decision allowed us to compare the neurochemical responses of those who donated to those who had not. Random neuro-chemical fluctuations are unlikely to correlate with behaviors like donating money.

We processed 580 tubes of blood: 4 tubes each for the 145

adults who participated in the experiment. The data showed that one-third of the participants donated money to St. Jude's, and nearly all of these had watched the emotional video. A few people even gave all of their earnings to St. Jude's. Donations were given when participants' brains increased both cortisol and oxytocin. In the brain, the attentional response comes from the brain's release of dopamine, part of the brain's "wanting" system that orients us to things in our environment that may be of value. Dopamine is an excitatory neurotransmitter and causes an increase in arousal hormones like cortisol in the peripheral nervous system. In addition to the dopaminergic attentional response, oxytocin release produced empathy for Ben and his father.

These neurochemical responses map fairly closely onto the elements of persuasion in Aristotle's *Rhetoric*. Dopamine is similar to *logos,* as it generates attention to a story, and oxytocin corresponds to *pathos,* the awakening of emotion. The data showed that if only one of these neurochemicals changed, no donation was made. It was their joint effect that appeared to drive the decision to donate. The unemotional video of Ben and his father at the zoo did not change either neurochemical; nor did it change any of the half-dozen other neurochemicals we measured.

I should mention that we sent the money people donated to St. Jude's—it would be bad karma if we did not try to help kids with cancer after saying we would. Indeed, the Ben video is the most effective stimulus we have ever found to provoke the brain to release oxytocin, and over the years I have sent thousands of dollars in participant donations to St. Jude's. I have also shared the Ben video with many other researchers, and I remind them to include a donation decision and send the money to St. Jude's.

Our first experiment looking for extraordinary content was a partial success. The behavior of the fifty-one people who donated their blood money to St. Jude's showed that stories can be so compelling that they motivate people to take action. But maybe we were just lucky, or maybe the Ben video was special. We had to dig deeper.

## SCALING UP

We torture people just a little in our experiments, so asking them to part with the money they earned was a sneaky way to determine if an experience was extraordinary. Charities that seek to alleviate social ills use public service announcements (PSAs) to spread their messages. PSAs are widely available online, so we could use these in our next study and also include a donation decision. But popular PSAs have so many views on YouTube that I worried that participants' neurologic responses would be blunted. My team found a solution: we collected sixteen PSAs from Europe that we presumed US residents had not seen or had rarely seen. All were in English, focused on a social ill, and lasted either thirty or sixty seconds. None of the PSAs solicited donations.

Participants in the experiment could earn five dollars if they correctly answered a simple factual question about the video's content after watching it. For example, one of the questions asked, "Was there a car in this video?" We did this so that study participants would pay attention to the videos and so that donation decisions were based on money participants felt they had earned. Decades of research have shown that it is more difficult to donate money one has earned compared to gifted money. We matched a charity to each cause shown in the PSAs. All the charities were US-based to eliminate country bias. For example, after watching a Finnish PSA about heart disease, participants could donate their earnings to the American Heart Association. As with the St. Jude's video, we sent the money to each charity after the experiment was over.

The emotional content of the PSAs was quite varied; just a couple of them were sad like Ben's story. The Finnish PSA about heart disease showed people flying off an amusement-park ride to indicate their early deaths due to heart disease while goofy teenagers smirk in mock horror, signaling to the audience that the flying bodies are make-believe. A number of participants laughed when they watched it. Other PSAs used scarce tactics, like a UK video showing a horrific car wreck that warned against drunk driving.

The study was designed to minimize the pressure participants might feel to donate money. Each person had their identity hidden by being assigned a random number for their data, and all donation decisions were made by computer in private so people would not feel uncomfortable if they donated nothing. At the end of the study, a cashier who was not involved in the experiment discreetly paid participants their non-donated earnings in a sealed envelope. Donate or don't donate: it was a completely free choice.

The most unexpected finding from the experiment using the Ben video was the role of oxytocin. We needed to understand if oxytocin was the cause of donations, so in the PSA experiment we dosed participants with synthetic oxytocin before showing them the videos. A control group had a placebo squirted up their noses. Neither the participants nor the experimenters knew who received each substance; this is known as a "double-blind" study and eliminates unconscious tip-offs that might influence participants' behaviors.

The data showed that oxytocin dramatically impacted responses to the PSAs. Average donations were 56% higher for those who received oxytocin compared to participants who received the placebo. In addition, oxytocin-receiving participants donated to 50% more of the featured charities. The study was designed to figure out if and why oxytocin had an effect. Our analysis showed that participants given oxytocin were substantially more concerned about the characters featured in the PSAs. Oxytocin increased their empathy. Greater concern motivated more donations.

Reflecting on these findings, it is really quite odd that people donate at all. It is as if the brain is using a "monkey see, monkey do" approach to determine appropriate behaviors. Other studies from my lab have shown that the oxytocin effect is blunt: once oxytocin is increased, it affects a broad range of social behaviors. The brains of people who received synthetic oxytocin in this experiment seemed to be signaling, "Humans are really concerned about heart disease. You are a human, so you should be concerned too." Participants demonstrated their concern by donating money. Social creatures with social brains follow the herd. The data also revealed that participants understood that the stories in the PSAs were fictional even though the issues were real. Here is the disconnect: the donated money cannot help the actors in the videos out of their fictional binds. The money might help prevent the harm depicted in the PSAs from happening to an unknown other person, but this is a big "if." As in our previous studies, oxytocin motivated costly and tangible helping behaviors after people watched the videos.

The PSA experiment gave my group the confidence to continue scaling up and running studies to confirm our findings. In another experiment, we wanted to be sure that the European PSAs caused the brain to make its own oxytocin, as we found with the Ben video. So we took blood from forty-two people before and after they watched one of the PSAs. We measured the change in oxytocin and the change in a short-acting arousal hormone with a long name that is abbreviated ACTH. We wanted to test how quickly the attentional effect occurred, and ACTH changes more rapidly than our previous arousal signal, cortisol.

The blood confirmed our finding from the Ben video. When both ACTH and oxytocin increased after watching the PSA, donations were 261% higher than when only one or neither of these biomarkers changed. Our analysis showed that the brain's production of ACTH was associated with the amount of attention participants paid to the video, while oxytocin correlated with concern for the people in it.

We tentatively concluded that if you pay attention to a story and become emotionally engaged with the people in it, then the brain appears to be transported into the story's world. This is why your palms sweat when James Bond dodges bullets while you sit in a movie theater. It is also why you stifle a sniffle when Bambi's mother dies and why some PSAs cause people to donate money to a charity.

Now we had to figure out how attention and oxytocin interact with each other. To do this, we needed more equipment, more stories, and a lot of money.

## PERSUADING DARPA

Our scientific publications linking neurologic signals to people's actions were seen by a man who committed the US government to understanding what stories did in the brain. He was the same man who had invited me to the briefing at Quantico, retired Lt. Col. William (Bill) Casebeer. Bill was a program officer at the US Department of Defense's high-impact research division, known as DARPA, and has a PhD in philosophy with a focus on cognitive neuroscience and a couple of master's degrees. He was among the first generation of neurophilosophers, scholars who run neuroscience experiments to understand how philosophical principles and moral dilemmas are processed in the brain. My initial research on oxytocin examined moral behaviors as I described in my 2012 book *The Moral Molecule*, and Bill and I had worked on an experiment together before he worked at DARPA.

Program officers at DARPA serve three- to four-year terms and enter into the job proposing high-risk, high-reward research programs. DARPA only expects one in ten projects they fund to pay off because they are looking for "moonshots"—that is, projects that will radically change how the US military does its job. One of the moonshots that Bill created was called Narrative Networks, and the idea was brilliant: could special forces soldiers be trained to deploy a new superpower—storytelling?

Wait. What?

Bill thought that if scientists understood what stories do to the brain, then soldiers could be trained to use words rather than weapons to encourage people to cooperate with the US. He knew he'd have to get the science right before the US government would roll out such a program. The field of "narratology" was just developing, but it lacked scientific rigor and resources. Bill would change that.

To jumpstart his program, Bill offered "seed grants" to a number of labs working in related areas, including mine. This money gave us the opportunity to measure neural activity during stories in new ways and to relate this to people's actions. If our seed grant produced useful findings, we would receive more money to continue our studies. The goal of the Narrative Networks program was to reduce international conflict by improving communications. I loved this idea. We were off and running.

Bill challenged my lab to use technologies that were deployable to train soldiers at Fort Bragg, headquarters of the US Army Special Operations Command, and potentially in a theater of war. By this time, we had cataloged the neural responses to the Ben video using functional brain imaging and high-density electroencephalography (EEG), but both these approaches use large, expensive, and delicate machines that are not field-deployable. We needed something small, portable, and maybe even wireless.

Before we go any further, we have to take a short neuro-anatomy detour. Oxytocin receptors are found in the brain or *central nervous system* and also outside the brain in the *peripheral nervous system*. Peripherally, densities of oxytocin receptors are found on the heart and on one of the primary nerve bundles that connects the central and peripheral nervous systems, the vagus nerve. *Vagus* means "wanderer" in Latin, and the early anatomists showed that this longest of the nerves coming out of the head wanders to the heart and gut. The brain controls the functioning of the body using a set of "speed up" and "slow down" signals known as the *sympathetic* and *parasympathetic* branches of the nervous system. In this usage, *sympathetic* is not related to emotions but to an acceleration of arousal; cortisol and ACTH are associated with activity in the sympathetic nervous system. Oxytocin, on the other hand, activates the parasympathetic system, which calms people by reducing arousal. These neurologic "gas" and "brake" systems function without conscious control as our brains tune responses to our environment at millisecond frequency.

If you take a deep breath and hold it, your heart rate will slow. This is due to increased activity of the vagus nerve. When you were a child and your mother told you to take a few deep breaths to calm down, she was telling you how to activate the vagus nerve. Vagal activity can be measured using an electrocardiogram (ECG), the same equipment a doctor uses to check the functioning of your heart. My lab started measuring vagal responses to see if we could develop a noninvasive way to measure the oxytocin.

One more nerdy detour. Quantifying activity of the vagus nerve requires running raw cardiac data through several mathematical transformations. This turns out to be another "signal extraction" problem. The mathematics of signal extraction we used were developed during WWII to determine if radar signals were coming from enemy airplanes rather than clouds or birds. We wrote computer code to automate these processing steps, but trained research assistants were still needed to review the inputs and outputs to be sure the algorithms were working properly. Ensuring the analysis was done right meant that signal processing would take us a couple of months for every experiment we ran.

Our initial tests relating vagal tone to changes in oxytocin in blood failed. We couldn't afford sufficiently high-quality equipment to extract the signal from the brain's other activities. Enter DARPA funding. This money let us purchase a medical-grade ECG that used wireless sensors with a fifteen-foot range between the human participant and the base station receiving the data. We were getting closer to a field-deployable technology. Our first key finding was that vagal activity and the change in oxytocin in blood were positively correlated. The equipment let us measure the vagal response up to 250 times per second, giving us a rich data source from which we could build models to predict what people would do. We also correlated the attentional response to several changes in the peripheral nervous system, including an increase in palmar sweat and a rise in heart rate from its resting value.

I knew I could accelerate the pace of discovery if I had more funding to hire additional researchers and run more experiments. Unexpectedly, support from the US intelligence community's research agency, the Intelligence Advanced

Research Projects Activity (IARPA), was approved. The IARPA money allowed us to purchase all the equipment we needed to measure around 150 signals from the central and peripheral nervous systems simultaneously to develop a comprehensive rendering of how stories and experiences transport us to other worlds—all without needles or pain.

We discovered that the brain first switches on attention, and—depending on the person and the experience we created—the emotional response might be mighty or mild. If an experience does not capture attention in the first fifteen seconds, it is unlikely to do so at all. If, after the experience captures attention, there is a social component to it, particularly one involving conflict or fear, then oxytocin is likely to be released. This can be summarized as: first get my attention, then give me a reason to care about what I'm experiencing.

The neurologic state that motivates action after an experience involves rapid switching between the sympathetic and parasympathetic branches of the nervous system. This is a peculiar physiologic state and we needed a way to succinctly describe the confluence of attention and emotional resonance. We settled on the term *Immersion* because the neural response seems to transport people to new worlds. When Immersion is high, people become absorbed in the experience and enjoy it.

Immersive experiences that drive actions are easily remembered. Contrasting the brain activity of people who took an action after an experience ("responders") versus those who did not ("nonresponders") is the foundation of Immersion. Taking an action reveals that the experience was meaningful. You can think of Immersion like tension. If an experience generates high Immersion, people's brains are full of tension. Those in such a state want to dissipate neural tension by donating to charity or, as we will see in subsequent chapters, purchasing a product or sharing the experience on social media. Immersion has this effect because emotional experiences are tagged by the brain as important. Indeed, the brain stores emotional memories in a special way so they are easily accessed. This is why it is easy to remember the birth of your child, or when you met your wife on a plane, or horrible events like 9/11. Immersion is tension in your skull.

My lab's discovery of Immersion gave the US military a framework to understand and improve its communications. Immersion is a "leading indicator" of responses to the explicit or implicit call to action in messages the military releases. The military, or any organization creating messages, can increase the number of people who take an action by measuring neural responses and then editing the message to increase Immersion. The cycle of creating, measuring, editing, and measuring again was new to government communication specialists, but it is simply the scientific method applied to stories and experiences. The key is knowing what to measure in the brain rather than relying on intuition or self-reports.

## GETTING IN THE GAME

The most important word in science is *bullshit*. Scientists are trained to be skeptical. Of everything. Especially of their own findings. This is why experiments must be replicated: maybe a scientist was just lucky in her experiment, or maybe the participants in the experiment were special in some way, or maybe it was sunny or cloudy, or some other factor affected the results.

A good "gut check" in science is to see if you can replicate someone else's results. I decided we had better do this before we went too far down the Immersion rabbit hole.

*USA Today* is a national newspaper that for several decades has asked its readers to rate the commercials played during the Super Bowl. Airing a commercial during the Super Bowl is among the most expensive advertising a company can do. Boatloads of money are spent on Super Bowl commercials because so many people will see them. When Steve Jobs was the CEO of Apple, he oversaw and funded perhaps the most famous TV commercial ever, titled "1984." This sixty-second Ridley Scott–directed ad depicted IBM as Big Brother controlling the personal computer market and enforcing Orwellian groupthink through its dominance. The ad teased the upcoming release of the Apple Macintosh computer, saying that "1984 won't be like *1984*." Apple, then struggling to pay its bills, only had enough money to broadcast the ad a single time during the 1984 Super Bowl.

There are also famous Super Bowl commercial fails. These include salacious ads for website hosting company GoDaddy, culturally insensitive ads by Groupon and SalesGenie, a very odd ad about peeing by TaxAct, and an Outpost.com ad in which what appear to be live gerbils are fired from a cannon. I thought a good test of the predictive ability of Immersion would be to see if Immersion lined up with *USA Today*'s Super Bowl commercial ratings. Easy peasy.

Two days after the 2014 Super Bowl, before people's brains were saturated by re-airings of commercials, we measured Immersion while sixteen people watched Super Bowl ads in random order. It took my team three weeks to process the neurologic data. Then we compared the results to the *USA Today* ratings and found...zero correlation between neurologic Immersion and how much *USA Today* readers said they liked the ads. I had failed.

Clearly, I had to find some other research to do because my "gut check" did not work out.

I woke up the next morning at three o'clock, going through all the details. Maybe the machines were not properly calibrated. Maybe the data processing algorithms had errors. Maybe the people we tested were insane. My BS meter was pointing at a high value, but all was not lost. Time for a mulligan.

Redoing the study could tell us what we had done wrong. Since it seems like every commercial that has ever aired is on YouTube, we got the *USA Today* rankings for the 2013 Super Bowl and downloaded the relevant commercials. Once the machines were recalibrated and the algorithms checked, we recruited sixteen new participants to watch the 2013 Super Bowl commercials while we measured their neurologic responses.

The result: exactly the same. There was no relationship between neurologic Immersion and the self-reported "liking" of ads reported by *USA Today*. We also asked each participant in our experiment if they thought each ad was "persuasive" and if they were likely to purchase the advertised product.

None of this consciously reported information had any relationship to what had immersed their brains.

We were looking for confirmatory evidence that we would never find.

## ACTIONS OR LIKING

Using expensive medical-grade machines and processing reams of data with complex algorithms is not easy. Why not just ask people how immersed they are in an experience? That would be so much simpler.

Here's the science: the "liking" question asks people to reveal their emotional states. Even though the brain produces language, it cannot accurately reveal its unconscious emotional responses. Most people suffer from a Freudian hangover thinking that if one digs enough, the unconscious will reveal itself. It just ain't so. Consciously querying the unconscious is like asking your liver to report how much it enjoyed the hamburger you ate for lunch. You might guess at a number between one and ten, but almost no one would take that value seriously. Unconscious neural responses reside in a different space than consciousness and the two seldom meet—even if it seems like they should. I had fallen into the Freudian trap, trying to relate Immersion to self-reported "liking." Our brains do not give us access to unconscious emotional responses with any degree of accuracy.

The Immersion algorithm was developed to predict actions, not feelings. The test I should have run was to use Immersion to predict the increase in sales following Super Bowl commercials. Unfortunately, companies seldom report these data so I had to find a proxy. The best proxies were YouTube views of the ads and the number of YouTube comments. YouTube data are actions—people were doing something that was objectively measurable, generating the "buzz" of the commercials.

This new approach found a positive correlation between Immersion and both YouTube metrics for every one of the five years that we have run the Super Bowl study. The values for 2018 are typical: the correlation between Immersion and YouTube views is 0.27, and the correlation between Immersion and YouTube comments is 0.25. This means that commercials with higher Immersion receive more YouTube views and comments; Immersion causes people to take action.

Compare this to how well the *USA Today* ratings predict actions. "Liking" has a consistently negative relationship with YouTube views and comments: the correlations from the 2018 Super Bowl are −0.33 and −0.38. In plain language, this means that Super Bowl commercials that are "liked" generate less buzz. This is another nail in the self-report coffin. We'll discuss the predictive accuracy of Immersion in more detail in Chapter 3, but for now you should be skeptical of "liking" as a predictive measure.

### SUPER-IMMERSION

Our analysis of the 2018 Super Bowl commercials showed that Diet Coke's "Groove" was the most immersive of sixty-five ads we tested. Yes, you have permission to stop reading and watch it. If you watched "Groove," you probably agree that it is not a "likable" commercial. In fact, *USA Today* readers ranked it dead last for "likability" among that year's Super Bowl commercials. This thirty-second spot shows a very tall and rather odd young woman talking about Diet Coke Twisted Mango and then dancing. She is filmed asymmetrically against a bright yellow wall and her dancing is weirdly uncoordinated. The woman and filming are so odd that it is hard to look away. Immersion for this commercial was four standard deviations above the advertising benchmark (in human-speak, that means the brain response was very powerful). The data also show that the Diet Coke branding at the commercial's end occurs during an Immersion peak, effectively linking the neural response to the brand.

Let's contrast this with what *USA Today* readers said they "liked" the most in 2018. On top of the list was a commercial for Amazon. Amazon splurged on a ninety-second commercial titled "Alexa Loses Her Voice," spending $16 million for air time alone. The ad features movie and music stars "filling in" for Alexa, including Anthony Hopkins and Cardi B. Stars do not work cheap, so the total cost of this commercial could easily be double what Amazon paid for air time. Our analysis showed it ranked ninth for Immersion, not a bad showing. But the second-by-second Immersion data show how it could have been better. Immersion during "Alexa Loses Her Voice" plummets starting at second thirty and stays low through second ninety. This happens because the commercial reuses the same pattern in all five scenes: someone asks Alexa a question and a famous star answers it inappropriately. Every time. By the second iteration, the brain understands the pattern, so repeating it dampens Immersion.

Here is the business case: if Amazon had used only the first thirty seconds of "Alexa Loses Her Voice," Immersion would have increased by 15%. This would have made it the second-most immersive Super Bowl commercial in 2018, putting more tension into viewers' brains and generating a greater desire to purchase an Amazon virtual assistant. Doing this would not only drive up the impact of the commercial, but it would have saved Amazon $10 million on air time. Immersive content and experiences are more memorable, more meaningful, and—as we will see in the next chapters—they powerfully drive sales. Amazon lost money and impact by failing to measure what matters.

We found another "liking" anomaly in Super Bowl commercials. If the commercial showed a puppy or a baby, its "liking" rating was high. Have you ever wondered why there are puppies in toilet paper commercials? It is focus group mania. Really, what kind of person would say that they do not "like" an ad with a baby or puppy in it? Our analysis showed that unless the puppy or baby is part of the narrative of the commercial, adding a gratuitous cute creature does not raise Immersion.

The brain is not fooled.

## GETTING SMALL

Measuring brain activity from a limited number of people to predict broad market outcomes has been called "neuro-forecasting." Up to this point, my group used delicate and expensive instruments to measure Immersion. We purchased $500 superduty Pelican cases to ship them to field-study sites around the US. These instruments could be sent to Afghanistan or Iraq to help the US military improve messages, but honestly, they would not last long bumping across dirt roads in a Humvee. There was more work to do if we were to measure Immersion everywhere extraordinary experiences were happening.

We needed to engineer a technology that was portable, durable, and could measure Immersion the moment it was happening. First, we got rid of the expensive and delicate machines. Then we eliminated the PhDs needed to process the data. Really, who wants a gaggle of PhDs at their experience anyway? Then we needed a lot of people to collect a lot of data. This is why I and some former PhDs from my lab built the Immersion software platform. Immersion software lives in cloud servers and applies algorithms I wrote using cardiac data from smartwatches and fitness sensors to infer neural states in real time. We normalized Immersion data so it runs from zero to one hundred. Everyone can understand that an eighty is better than a forty. Pairing wearables with in-the-cloud processing meant that Immersion was fast and easy to measure and that anyone, not just my team of nerds, could do it.

Subscribers to the Immersion platform use it in ways I could not imagine. In the following chapters, I will tell you how Immersion identified top-rated TV shows and hit music months before release, how it predicted movie ticket sales, and even how it predicted which TV shows people wanted to watch during the COVID-19 quarantine. A major professional services company, Accenture, measures Immersion during the training they provide to employees to ensure all learners benefit. Immersion has even been used to help people find love and to repair marriages. The extensive use of the Immersion platform has identified key principles you can use to create extraordinary experiences. Improving the impact of advertising was one of the first uses of the Immersion platform, so we will learn how companies have done this in the next chapter.

**KEY TAKEAWAYS**

1. Immersion is a neurologic state in which one is attentive to an experience and it resonates emotionally.
2. Immersion predicts what people will do, not what they feel.
3. Emotional resonance drives most of the variation in Immersion during an experience.
4. Immersive experiences get top billing in the brain so they are easily remembered.
5. Immersion can be measured in real time by anyone using the Immersion software platform.

# CHAPTER 2

# ADVERTISING THAT PERSUADES

"I'm not gay, but I'd have sex with any of those guys." This is what a participant named "Liam" said in the middle of a study. I struggled to remain expressionless.

My team and I were measuring Immersion to see if people love products the same way they love other people.

This idea is not as crazy as it seems. Think of how you feel when you can't find your mobile phone. And be honest: Have you named your car? What's the story with that?!

I describe the brain as a lazy Republican. It is a Republican because it is conservative in how it expends energy. It is lazy because brain networks that evolved for one purpose activate for different purposes today. The brain's laziness means it does a quick cost-benefit analysis to see if it should expend metabolic resources on something it encounters. If the experience does not seem sufficiently valuable, few neural resources will be spent and the stimulus will be largely ignored. Bottom line: what we think our brains do and what they really do are quite different. This is why brain activity needs to be measured to understand what motivates people's actions rather than relying on self-reports of imagined mental processes. It also means that evolutionarily conserved brain networks may activate in unexpected circumstances.

The experiment that prompted the oversharing about gay sex asked participants to bring in a favorite product and a picture of a favorite person. Participants were instructed to tell me why they loved the product for sixty seconds while we measured Immersion. Then they would tell me for one minute why they loved the person. We wanted to know if people were just using fanciful language or if they had actually fallen in love with products.

The results surprised us.

One participant, "George," brought in a custom-made Wilson baseball mitt. He told me about playing in Little League and then in high school. When he was in college, he was a standout pitcher, earning a starting position as a freshman. The mitt reminded him of the great times he had at games with his teammates, going on road trips, and the crazy things that happened to him. We took a ninety-second break to allow his brain to return to baseline. Then I asked him about the picture he'd brought. It was of his girlfriend. They were moving in together that weekend and "would probably get married." I didn't need to see George's neurologic data to know he was not excited about this. George's shoulders dropped, his voice dropped, and his eyes dropped. The data showed that George was 300% more immersed in the stories provoked by his baseball mitt than he was in his girlfriend.

Most people in the study were not like George. Averaging across all participants, Immersion was 54% higher when talking about people compared to products. What product was most loved? More than half the participants brought in mobile phones. Overall, the proportion of Immersion due to attention and emotional resonance was nearly identical for people and products, indicating that similar pathways were active in the lazy Republican brain.

Liam was an outlier. He was British and had brought in a scarf from his favorite football (soccer) team, Manchester United. He passionately described how, since he was a teen, he would meet his mates at the stadium, get drunk and rowdy, and have loads of fun during games. Now that he lived in the US, he watched Manchester United at a beachside pub and said his "wife better watch out if they lose" because he would be irritable for days. This is when he blurted out, in a room full of scientists, that although he was straight, he would have sex with Manchester United players.

After a ninety-second break, he showed me the picture of his most loved person, his two-year-old daughter, "Melissa." His face lit up when he talked about her, but he used mostly general language like "cute" and "sweet." His Immersion was 55% higher for Manchester United than it was for Melissa. I am sure he loved his daughter, but he had not had a chance to build up experiences with her as he had during Manchester United matches.

Here's the kicker for marketers: one-third of people we tested were more immersed in the product they brought in than in their most loved person. All the product-people had one thing in common: a rich and emotional set of stories about the product.

We say, "I love that movie" or "I can't live without my phone," using exactly the same words we use about people, not only because of our limited vocabulary to express feelings. The lazy Republican brain uses similar evolutionarily conserved brain networks when valuing people, products, and experiences. This is why Immersion can be used to measure romantic relationships and, as we will discuss in this chapter, make kick-ass advertising.

## STUCK IN THE DRIVEWAY

Several decades ago, National Public Radio realized the power of stories when they received messages from listeners who could not leave their cars until the broadcast was over. NPR calls these "driveway stories" because people sit in their cars in front of their homes listening to the radio. This aural hostage-taking is an objective indicator of the power of immersive stories.

My team and I were intrigued by the idea of driveway stories, but getting people to linger in their driveways during an experiment was logistically impossible. Instead, we focused on commercials. Commercials are short narratives that are ideal for experiments because they have objective outcomes. Companies evaluate advertising by tracking purchases, social media shares, and recall of branding. Unless Immersion predicted these types of observable outcomes, it would not create value for marketers. After my team's research received media coverage, companies started asking for our help. This gave us a chance to measure why advertising works or fails.

A major US life insurance company knew it had to change its TV commercials but was unsure which direction to take. The commercials they were airing featured an expert who intoned, "Make sure you plan for a long life." There was no mention of death or obligations, and the imagery used was squarely focused on married men with families. This trope had been effective for decades because married men were the traditional purchasers of life insurance. But today, women make the majority of household financial decisions, and the company needed our help to determine how to advertise to women. And, since we were testing new content, could we also figure out what would influence young men to purchase life insurance?

My team collected neurologic and behavioral data from 178 people who viewed unbranded rough cuts of video and print advertising for life insurance. Participants earned at least $75,000 per year, most were married, and nearly all had let their life insurance lapse. These parameters ensured we were testing people who would be interested in life insurance. We collected data in Chicago, Philadelphia, and Los Angeles and had a broad distribution of ages and ethnicities to ensure that our results generalized.

When the study concluded, participants were given the option of sharing their email addresses so a life insurance agent could call them. Even if they were curious about life insurance, most people would rather not have a salesperson call them. Yet one-third of participants gave us their emails. We included this decision as one of the objective measures of advertising effectiveness that we sought to predict; the emails were not shared with the company in order to compartmentalize research and sales.

Our analysis showed that those who shared their emails were the most immersed in the commercials. This remained true when we statistically removed the effects of marriage, children, and income. Our analysis showed that Immersion predicted participants' willingness to take a call from an insurance salesperson to consider purchasing life insurance. Immersion also predicted participants' recall of details of the commercials when we sent them a survey a week after the study and whether the participants had discussed life insurance with their families.

Neurologic data is valuable not only because it is objective, but also because it adds to traditional measures such as demographics to improve the predictive accuracy of marketing campaigns. The term of art for this is *orthogonal,* meaning that Immersion is unrelated to other data streams. Beyond that, Immersion is measured second-by-second so it can be used to edit advertisements to increase their influence. Traditional measures like demographics or "liking" are not granular.

We combined demographic information and Immersion to help the insurance company more effectively differentiate itself from its competitors—something all insurance companies struggle with. Our analysis revealed that as household income increased, so did Immersion. This makes sense financially: those who have more income have more to protect, so their brains were more immersed in the information we showed them.

This neurologic process is known as "top-down control." Executive centers in the brain allocate supplementary processing power when one encounters something that is relevant. For example, neural activation is greater when a smoker sees a pack of cigarettes than when a nonsmoker sees one. Nicotine is highly rewarding to smokers so the brain devotes more resources to processing information about cigarettes. More generally, top-down control generates higher Immersion for experiences if they are important to the individual. This is why Immersion was elevated in high-income participants watching life insurance commercials. In fact, we found high Immersion in the richest participants for every single commercial and print advertisement we tested. *Relevance increases Immersion.* This is known as the "targeting problem" in marketing, sending a tailored message to different market segments. Measuring neural responses helps marketers identify the most immersive message for different market participants.

We also used the Immersion data to identify the types of content and emotional tone of messages that were most immersive to participants by sex, marital status, and age. These insights gave the company a blueprint they took to their ad agency to guide the development of new advertising campaigns. We did not have to ask people their opinions; their brains revealed how to get them to care about life insurance.

Immersion data sometimes produces a d'oh moment where

we see something completely obvious. This is a good "gut check" and ensures that the results make sense. We found that only a single commercial produced Immersion above the advertising benchmark in young men. In this video, a male motorcycle rider is talking to the camera from the side of the road. The viewer sees his motorcycle underneath a car. As the rider speaks, the viewer gradually understands that he has died and is sharing his regret that he cannot provide for his daughter because he did not have life insurance. This fear appeal was only immersive in young males; all other demographic segments were neurologically turned off by this commercial. Relevance matters for Immersion.

## PEAKING INTEREST

In order to show the life insurance company how to improve its commercials, I created a measure that quantifies the length and depth of high Immersion moments. I call this "peak Immersion." This metric gives content creators a tool to improve an experience by modifying it so the peaks are higher and last longer. Imagine a commercial showing a little boy on a swing by himself that generates moderate Immersion. Immersion can be raised by showing this scene for a longer period of time or by adding in music that accentuates the loneliness the boy feels. The peak Immersion metric is an important check to ensure that raising Immersion at one point does not reduce peaks at other times—something that could drag down overall Immersion.

There is an old saying about investing in the stock market: let your winners run and cut your losses early. This logic should be applied to creating immersive advertising. An experience will have more impact when peak Immersion moments are allowed to run. Similarly, editing out periods of neural disengagement when Immersion flags will raise overall Immersion. More succinctly, this means more good stuff and less bad stuff. When creative agencies do this, Immersion rises and market impact is higher.

Editing content to raise peak Immersion has a second effect. As we discussed in Chapter 1, the most memorable parts of an experience are moments of high emotion and what happens at the end. Branding is more likely to be remembered when it occurs at an Immersion peak. This is especially important for poorly differentiated products like life insurance. Advertisers get a recall double whammy when an Immersion peak occurs at the end of a commercial. Quantifying peak Immersion showed the insurance company how to craft their commercials to produce an emotional climax at the conclusion in order to lodge the company's name into viewers' memories.

Over the years, I have reviewed Immersion for more than one hundred life insurance commercials. The data show that company branding rarely occurs during Immersion peaks. Rather, the branding is almost always shown at the end of a commercial, often when Immersion is trailing off as narrative tension resolves. Peak Immersion will increase branding recall at any point in an advertisement; one need not wait until the commercial ends to display a logo and a call to action. Branding can also be done more than once, even in a thirty-second commercial. Suppose the middle of a commercial has an Immersion peak when insurance agents are shown assisting homeowners after a house fire. The scene will reinforce recall of the company if it includes, for example, a company-branded vehicle. The Immersion peak could also be extended showing the agent helping her clients for a longer period of time. Close-ups of faces also spike Immersion, so the camera should linger on the face of the relieved homeowner in order to raise overall Immersion. If branding is only done at the end, creatives should ensure there is an Immersion peak to capture the peak-end double whammy.

I describe the process of measuring Immersion during the content creation process as "Creative+." Immersion does not replace content creators; rather, it objectively guides them through each stage, from dialogue, to storyboards, to rough cuts, to music, and on to the final edit. Neural measures inform the creative process by showing where and how to refine and enhance content for maximum market impact. Without content and those who create it, there is no measurement and nothing to improve.

## SUPERFANS

Around 12% of participants in the original life insurance study had Immersion levels that were through the roof. I call these ecstatic people "superfans." Nearly all of the superfans provided their emails so they could be contacted by a life insurance agent. Finding superfans is easy—they are Immersion outliers, no self-report needed. Later research by my group showed that superfans are the most likely to share brand information on social media. Identifying these impassioned individuals provides powerful leverage to marketers because they spread advertising messages even without being asked to do so.

My team and I wanted to know if neurologic superfans just randomly arose or if they could be created.

We designed a study in which seventy-seven men and women completed a standard scale to evaluate their relationship with a dozen popular brands that sold computer memory sticks, reusable water bottles, and headphones. A week later, participants were intranasally infused with either 40 IU (international units) of synthetic oxytocin or a placebo using a double-blind protocol after having given written consent and passing a medical screening. Since oxytocin is the primary driver of Immersion, I thought it might create an army of superfans. After the intranasal infusion, participants were exposed to brand information from the companies' websites. My team then determined how much participants would pay for each product using a set of *yes* or *no* questions. We also asked them to write down their feelings about each brand.

My hypothesis was correct: oxytocin caused a surge in brand attachment. Oxytocin-treated participants said the brands they were exposed to were much better compared to those who received a placebo. Importantly, superfans were willing to pay more for the headphones, memory sticks, and water bottles. When writing about brands, oxytocin-fueled superfans used substantially more positive emotional terms and language about relationships compared to their placebo brethren. A number of control conditions showed that oxytocin participants were cognitively intact; the oxytocin had simply created superfans for the brands they had been shown. Confirming our earlier study, we found that oxytocin was the neural substrate for the love of both brands and people.

Of course, outside the lab, superfans emerge without being drugged. I take that back; their brains' own release of oxytocin has "drugged" them so they fall in love with a commercial or brand. Marketers can do this by creating immersive brand stories and then inviting superfans to share them. Think how hard Liam, the Manchester United superfan, would work to help his team if he were asked. The takeaway is not that you should spritz your store with synthetic oxytocin, which would clearly be immoral and illegal, but that advertising and customer experiences should seek to build emotional attachments to brands. When brands do this, customers will be loyal brand ambassadors and will be happy to pay for the brand's products. It is a formula worth using: emotion increases Immersion increases sales.

Scrutinizing brain responses to thousands of pieces of content provided the data to build a profile of superfans. My team discovered that superfans score high on two personality traits: empathy and agreeableness. These folks have warm personalities and want to please others. In technical terms, these wonderful humans have high "affect intensity." They express heartfelt emotions and tend to have a lot of friends. About 60% of these warm people are women. Knowing that personality traits affect neural activity allows one to create demographic and psychographic profiles of superfans so they can be encouraged to engage with the brand after viewing advertising.

Think of the love and loyalty that Apple and Disney engender and how much Liam loved Manchester United. Just like love for people, love for brands needs to be nurtured. Superfans can be identified demographically and then targeted with advertising on their favorite cable channels, magazines, or radio programs; or they can be micro-targeted using online content. Superfans are so valuable that companies should establish special offers and loyalty programs customized for them.

Once superfans are identified demographically, companies need to give them something to do. Now. Ask them to click on a link, share with others, purchase, talk, or create fan fiction. Give them a way to dissipate the immersive tension brand exposure has put into their brains. Failing to engage superfans is inexcusable because it is so easy to find them: they are the ones spreading the word about an ad or brand. Ask them to post a review on Yelp or Amazon, send them a logo sticker to put on their cars, or ask them for the email address of a friend that the company should contact. Superfans see themselves as part of the brand's "family." That is oxytocin at work, building attachment. This is not manipulative: superfans want to be associated with the brand. They can say no if they would rather not help. But the data show they do want to help and will. Social proof is a powerful marketing approach, and superfans willingly provide social proof to their networks.

## CALIFORNIA INDIFFERENCE

Elie Wiesel once said, "The opposite of love is not hate, it is indifference." A study we did for the state of California showed that commercials that produce indifference are guaranteed to fail. But some value can still be obtained from them.

California, like most US states, created an online marketplace offering health insurance plans after the 2010 passage of the

Affordable Care Act. By the second year of the program, health insurance purchases in California were well below what was expected. This surprised policy-makers, since those who had not purchased health insurance would face a penalty imposed by the Internal Revenue Service. The penalty revenue would subsidize the purchase of health insurance by lower-income households.

The state paid one of the "Big Four" ad agencies $150 million to create and air TV commercials hectoring Californians to purchase health insurance. The commercials did not seem to have any effect on consumers, and the state asked us to figure out why. My team recruited eighty-five Californians to watch commercials for the California health insurance exchange while we measured Immersion. Participants watched commercials in their preferred language; roughly one half chose English, and the other half chose Spanish.

Conspicuous in the data was the low Immersion for all the commercials. The second-by-second data showed this was due to the lack of a narrative structure; there was no conflict and no reason to care about the characters. In fact, as the commercials progressed, Immersion plunged. Half of the commercials failed to show the actors' faces, the primary way we share emotions. Faces nearly always need to be part of effective advertising.

The data also revealed a relevance problem. Identical commercials were aired with voice-overs in English and Spanish, presumably to save the cost of producing different messages. We discovered that Spanish speakers watching commercials in Spanish were, on average, 70% less immersed than were

English speakers watching in English. Our analysis showed that this effect was not due to income differences, or time of day, or other factors. Instead, we traced the low Immersion to story context. The commercials featured the ethnic diversity of California: African Americans, Asians, Caucasians, and Hispanics were all shown. As a result, the settings and narratives were generic, showing scenes of daily life like shopping for groceries or riding a bike.

Generic commercials inevitably use the iconography of the dominant culture. For example, one commercial, called "Taco," showed an ethnically diverse group of people picking out tacos at a chain-style Mexican restaurant while the voice-over explained that just like people prefer different types of tacos, they also prefer different health plans. Great. Except Hispanics in California are not fans of eating tacos at Americanized chain restaurants. Either their mama makes tacos at home or they hit an authentic hole-in-the-wall Mexican food joint. For Hispanics, the inauthenticity of the setting drove down Immersion. No Immersion, no action. The brain evaluates the relevance of experiences, and Immersion responds accordingly.

Since Immersion was measured second-by-second, we could analyze whether threats of penalties were effective at motivating insurance purchases. Half of the commercials ended with "Sign up now to avoid the IRS penalty," and the other half ended with "Call for free help." Immersion fell for the threat but increased for the offer of free help. Free is good, and free help is even better.

We questioned participants a week after they had watched

the commercials to see what effects they'd had. The few high-Immersion participants remembered that the ads were for the California health insurance exchange and visited the California health insurance website. The handful of superfans had been persuaded by the commercials and had signed up for health insurance.

We advised the state to target specific segments of the population with different messages. These messages needed to have a crisis and emotions, and to illustrate how easy, inexpensive, and important it is to have health insurance. This sounds like Marketing 101, but without testing, California bureaucrats were depending on their intuition and the intuition of their ad agency—intuition that burned $150 million of taxpayer money with little effect.

## HIDDEN RELEVANCE

How do you tell an immersive story when consumers never see your product? A major computer chip maker wanted to know how well their ad agency was telling their story. The company had identified three market segments that cared about the type of chip in computers and mobile devices. All three sets of consumers were pretty nerdy, and we wanted to figure out what kind of message immersed nerds in semiconductor minutiae.

We recruited seventy people in the target demographic and asked them to watch eight of the company's commercials while we collected neurologic data. Immersion for most of the videos was around the advertising benchmark, no big winners in the bunch, and two of them were plain awful.

Department store pioneer John Wanamaker famously said, "Half the money I spend on advertising is wasted; the trouble is, I don't know which half." Immersion identified which half of the advertising had the largest market impact. That is a solid step forward for any advertiser. The best ads for the semiconductor company showed people happily using technology, and some featured a famous nerdy actor. The ads were relevant to the target population.

Across the three audience segments, average Immersion was nearly identical for all the commercials. But the distribution of superfans varied substantially across the commercials. Stay with me here because this point is important but subtle. A well-structured story will produce high Immersion in nearly everyone: neurologically, a good story is a good story is a good story. But when stories are mediocre, the differences in Immersion across demographic segments tend to be small. In this case, superfans have an oversized effect on average Immersion.

The semiconductor commercial with the highest Immersion also had the most superfans, but even the weaker ads had people whose brains loved the story. When we contacted participants a week after watching the ads, Immersion predicted recall of the company and a perception of the company as innovative. As expected, superfans remembered more details about the commercials and said they were influenced by the information. An average commercial can still move markets if there are enough superfans who love it.

As with health insurance messages, we advised the semiconductor company to create different messages for different users.

We also suggested that they forget broadcast media that seeks to tell a generic story to people who are mostly uninterested in computer chips. Instead, they should create, test, and stream ads that are relevant to an identified group of customers and ride the long tail of superfandom. Not only do superfans have a preference for the company's products, but they are highly motivated to proselytize on the company's behalf. This is true even when they cannot see the product being advertised.

## BUZZ AND BLINDED LIONS

Immersion is only useful if it predicts market outcomes. My skeptical science brain was still concerned that we had gotten lucky when we used Immersion to predict outcomes. In order to really establish Immersion's predictive power, we had to measure Immersion without knowing which commercials were best. Two companies gave us a chance to do this.

An insurance company collaborated with my group to measure the Immersion of TV commercials showing how the company responded to natural disasters. The company used YouTube views as their measure of market buzz. One month after we measured Immersion in five commercials, they were released online. Immersion nearly perfectly predicted YouTube views, a 0.82 correlation that was statistically meaningful. This was a surprisingly strong relationship since the highest-Immersion commercial had more than sixty thousand views, while the commercial with the lowest Immersion had fewer than three thousand. Such large spreads are typically hard to predict, yet we were able to do it.

As a double-check, I added in a second measure to predict:

donations to charities focused on disaster relief, replicating what my group had done with the video of the boy dying of cancer. Again, there was a statistically significant high correlation between Immersion and charitable donations, 0.72. That people chose to donate at all shows the power of immersive stories. Study participants had to drive to a hotel, have a sensor put on their arms, and sit in a conference room for an hour while they watched commercials, and yet some of them still felt compelled to donate money.

Predicting buzz was one thing, but I really wanted to predict advertising-influenced purchases. I just didn't know how to get these data.

I have a web crawler that tracks the word *oxytocin*. In 2014 it picked up a video from Cannes, France. Major media purchases for advertising happen annually at a meeting called Cannes Lions. It is held the week before the more famous Cannes Film Festival. The video my web crawler found featured Josy Paul, chairman of the Indian division of the global advertising agency BBDO. In his presentation, Mr. Paul said that BBDO's ads were so creative that "they caused the brain to make oxytocin." I was intrigued. And skeptical. I had developed the delicate procedure to measure the brain's acute production of oxytocin using blood draws. Had BBDO really done this?

After twenty minutes of searching, I found a memo with Mr. Paul's email. My message to him asked how BBDO had measured oxytocin and said that if they really wanted to do this, I was interested. Two hours later, I got a reply that basically said, "Holy crap, you're Paul Zak; we want to talk to you." Mr. Paul connected me to BBDO Asia's head of strategy, Andy Wilson. I explained that Immersion, not just oxytocin, was the best predictor of market outcomes and that I could measure it with wireless sensors. "Okay," he said, "let's see how well it predicts." But Wilson set the prediction bar significantly higher than in our previous studies. We would have to predict blindly.

Here's how it went. Wilson sent me eighteen TV commercials that BBDO had created for six different brands. There were three commercials each for Snickers candy bars, Cesar dog food, AT&T phone services, Visa credit cards, and two beers—Guinness and Bud Light. The blind prediction was made more difficult because BBDO's clients had ranked the commercials by sales bumps, but each company had used their own methodology. BBDO would withhold the sales bump rankings from us while we measured each commercial for Immersion.

A blind prediction is the ultimate test of accuracy because there is no way to cherry-pick the data or do esoteric statistical analyses to improve the forecast: either Immersion predicts sales or it does not. Honestly, my team was itching to solve the Wanamaker problem and be certain that Immersion could identify messages that would drive up sales.

We recruited sixty-one participants to watch BBDO's commercials while we measured Immersion. Respondents, who ranged from college students to the middle-aged, were balanced by gender and had varying ethnicities and incomes.

The results? Immersion correctly identified the commercials that produced the largest sales bump for five of the six brands. This meant Immersion predicted sales with 83% accuracy and the result was statistically reliable. Here's another way to understand our findings: there is a statistically significant linear relationship between Immersion and sales bumps, so as Immersion increases, so do sales.

Josy Paul was correct: BBDO's commercials did cause oxytocin release, and they also prompted dopamine release that captured attention. BBDO's blind test was the best evidence that neural signals from a modest number of individuals accurately predict market responses. Brain as predictor indeed.

You must be wondering which brand our forecast missed. It was Bud Light. Andy Wilson later told me that Bud Light had, in addition to airing TV commercials, sponsored live concerts, run a social media campaign, and done swag giveaways that affected sales but that our analysis was unable to capture because we only had data from the commercials. BBDO had thrown us a red herring. The neurologic data did what it was designed to do: predict the impact of communications and ignore red herrings.

Our analysis of the three Guinness commercials revealed an important aspect of persuasive messages that I call product-story congruence. I touched on this briefly when I discussed how the California health insurance commercials failed to immerse Hispanic viewers. Let's go deeper into this topic by contrasting two of the Guinness commercials we tested: "Barnes Sisters" and "Empty Chair."

"Barnes Sisters" is a perfectly simple story. The camera slowly pans in on a black-and-white photo of twins who are Olympic athletes. Text appears below each picture, saying, "Tracy

Barnes," "Lanny Barnes," then "Born April 26, 1982" "Born April 26, 1982," then "Became a biathlete," "Became a biathlete," then "Went to the games," "Went to the games," then "Came home empty handed," "Came home empty handed," then "Kept on training," "Kept on training," then "This year, one last chance," "This year, one last chance," then "At the final trial," "At the final trial." Now the pattern changes, something the brain loves. The next text reads "Qualified," then a pause, and below Lanny's picture the text says, "Was too ill to compete." Okay, we have a crisis. Next it says, "Tracy gave up her spot" "So Lanny could compete." This is the hero's journey on full display. The story has immersed us and then... The Guinness logo and tagline appear. The neurologic data showed that while the story had average Immersion, viewers were tuned out at the end, just when the branding was shown. The commercial went from a beautiful story to a blatant sales pitch to buy beer. "Barnes Sisters" had a moderate impact on sales because the story was moderately immersive until it took a dive during the last ten seconds of clumsy branding. I have imagined how logical the BBDO pitch of this concept to Guinness must have been: 80% of Guinness drinkers are male and everyone knows that men like women and sports, so this ad just had to work.

Contrast this with BBDO's "Empty Chair" commercial for Guinness. The story starts at an English pub where the barmaid is preparing to open. Before the patrons enter, she puts a glass of Guinness on a table. The glass stays there undrunk all night. Time speeds up and nights come and go as people enter the pub and enjoy themselves, and every evening a glass of Guinness is placed on a table with an empty chair. Every night the barmaid looks weary and worn. In one scene, a man tries to take the chair from the table with the Guinness. The woman offers a very gentle shake of her head and the man leaves the chair. We have a setting, we have a mystery, and we have conflict: Who is this woman? Who is she waiting for? Why doesn't someone drink that beer? Next, we see the barmaid light up the "Open" sign, pour a Guinness and place it on the same table with the empty chair. She is still weary. Then we are outside and the camera moves to show that we are walking toward the pub. The perspective changes to the inside of the busy pub, and we see a soldier in fatigues, carrying a full rucksack, open the door and step in. He looks around. The barmaid sees him and subtly nods her head at the table with the pint of Guinness. The soldier walks over, picks up the glass, and gives the woman a small, tired smile. Others in the pub see the soldier, and they lift their glasses of Guinness to salute him. Now we see the Guinness tagline and logo.

I'm such a softie; I teared up just writing this description of "Empty Chair." The commercial blew Immersion off the charts. It is one of the most immersive commercials among the thousands we have tested.

"Empty Chair" shows the intersection of two heroes' journeys: the barmaid and the soldier. Both are extraordinary by serving others even when they are exhausted. The implication of the commercial is that we, too, can be extraordinary by working hard and then rewarding ourselves with a Guinness. The product enters the story seamlessly, and the wordless narrative is inspiring. Guinness wants viewers to aspire to be the kind of people who support those who are in service to others. They might just show that support by drinking Guinness. "Barnes Sisters," on the other hand, just dropped in the

Guinness branding at the end of a pleasant story. It lacked the product-story congruence that was baked into "Empty Chair."

I need to modify my claim that neurologically a "good story is a good story is a good story." While not incorrect, if the goal of your story is to sell a product, then the product must be a natural part of a good story to sell successfully.

## FACING THE SMALL SCREEN

The ubiquity of online media means that nearly all TV commercials are released to sites like YouTube, Facebook, or Vimeo. Some Super Bowl commercials are released *before* the big day to build buzz. The proportion of people watching TV has been falling since 2005, so the impact of TV advertising is waning. TV viewers also skew older. TV viewing for the critical eighteen- to forty-nine-year-old demographic that spends money to keep up with the latest trends is now less than two hours a week. At the same time, personal computers are being replaced by portables, including tablet computers and smartphones. In the online world, people are inundated with advertisements. Estimates are that people see between six thousand and ten thousand ads every day and ignore them as much as possible. As a result, advertising's impact on purchases is in rapid decline. In 2018, the largest advertiser in the world, consumer products company Procter & Gamble, announced that they had cut their digital advertising spending by $200 million because they could not show it was effective. P&G cut their ad spend in 2019 by another $350 million. What is the world coming to?

Facebook earns 98% of its revenue from advertising and has

good reason to be concerned that its impact may be dwindling. A possible cause of advertising impotence is shrinkage—videos are increasingly viewed on small screens. Facebook asked my team to analyze whether Immersion of commercials watched on a mobile phone differs from those watched on a TV-sized monitor.

We recruited seventy people in the eighteen- to forty-nine-year-old demographic, equally split between men and women. Facebook asked us to measure the Immersion of three movie trailers (*The Fault in Our Stars, Entourage, Get Hard*) and a Victoria's Secret commercial. Participants watched videos on an iPhone 6 in the portrait (narrow) orientation and on a thirty-two-inch monitor. To make it realistic, the videos on the large monitor were shown during commercial breaks of popular TV shows. In the mobile phone condition, the commercials were included in Facebook's News Feed. Each person watched the videos twice: once on the phone and once on the monitor. The researchers at Facebook and I thought that videos watched on the iPhone would have lower Immersion than those watched on the monitor. The data proved otherwise... mostly.

Average Immersion for the four ads was 42% higher on the mobile phone than on the big screen. My team and the researchers at Facebook were pleasantly surprised. A week after the study, we contacted participants to see what they remembered. The data showed a strong positive relationship between Immersion and the content in the ads. As in our previous studies, immersive experiences are stored top of mind.

Analyzing each video, Immersion was higher on the small

screen compared to the big monitor for the Victoria's Secret commercial and two of the three movie trailers. Additional studies by our group confirmed that videos on phones are generally more immersive than those on a large monitor. One reason for this is that a phone must be held steady to watch a video. This creates somatic intimacy with the phone, becoming an extension of the body. A monitor, on the other hand, sits passively on the wall or desk.

So what happened with the movie trailer that was less immersive on the phone?

The trailers that were more immersive on the phone, *The Fault in Our Stars* and *Get Hard*, had a typical narrative structure. The *Entourage* trailer had a nonstandard structure resulting in low Immersion on both screens. Rather than developing a narrative arc, it used quick cuts of the actors in scenes that must have been familiar to those who watched the HBO series but confused most of the study participants as we discovered during debriefing. The trailer showed a random group of guys doing random things in Los Angeles. The *Entourage* video was also 52% longer than the other two trailers. By using quick cuts rather than developing characters, the *Entourage* trailer failed to create emotional resonance and Immersion plummeted. This was especially true for women who were 50% less immersed in this trailer than men were.

Our studies of Immersion on mobile devices shows that small is beautiful...and immersive. This is good news for Facebook, Google, and every company that advertises as mobile is now the dominant mode of content consumption.

## I WANT CANDY, BUT I'M NOT ADDICTED

Since I believe prediction is paramount, I have tested the predictive ability of Immersion in unusual ways. For example, we asked people to open and eat candies from their childhood while we measured Immersion. I wanted to know if Immersion could predict which candies people would purchase. A contact at a candy company was kind enough to send us boxes of their treats for our experiment. When the study was over, I had so many leftover Sour Punch candies and Red Vines that I brought them to my daughters' school and gave them away.

Consuming treats is not just about taste. It is also about sounds, smells, and memories. To capture all these effects, we measured Immersion while people looked at the candy in front of them, watched it being unwrapped, and then held it in their mouths for sixty seconds before chewing it or spitting it out.

You might be old enough to remember the 1971 song "Anticipation" by Carly Simon. Ms. Simon was onto something. The data showed that anticipation was the most immersive aspect of the candy experience. Immersion was almost 50% higher when people watched candy being unwrapped and when they picked it up compared to when they tasted it. Average Immersion during unwrapping and consumption predicted the candies people would buy with 78% accuracy. Even for something as individually variable as which candy one likes, Immersion predicted behaviors accurately. This level of accuracy is surprising because the company, not the participants, chose the candies.

While the high Immersion prior to consuming candies may surprise you, the neuroscience of this response is well known.

The brain system that orients us to rewards is driven by the release of the neurotransmitter dopamine as we discussed in Chapter 1. When the dopamine system does not work properly, people become pathologically apathetic and can even lose the will to live. Sometimes called "voodoo death" or "give-up-itis," it can happen to those in shipwrecks and to prisoners of war. Dopamine-driven attention is a necessary part of Immersion.

Effective marketing must engage the brain's wanting system. But not too much. When this system is out of control, addiction emerges. Addicts of all types—drugs, gambling, sex—tend to have underactive dopamine-driven wanting systems that generate cravings for their compulsion. Addicts are not satisfied when they get what they crave because dopamine is only weakly released during consumption. The anticipation of getting what they need stimulates dopamine. Dopamine diminishes cravings so people feel better. But because cravings recur, addicts are never satisfied. Sex without foreplay is quickly over, whereas the slow building of anticipation can make it last for hours. Sitting at a table in Las Vegas, smelling cigarette smoke, and sipping whiskey is foreplay for gambling addicts. Similarly, the brain links the high of drug use with people and places. When drug addicts avoid the cues associated with addictive behaviors, cravings are reduced.

It is important to emphasize that superfans are not shopping addicts. Many neuromarketing companies are obsessed with dopaminergic attention. The work from my lab definitely shows that attention is just the first step in motivating people to respond to advertisements. It is emotional resonance, the primary driver of Immersion, that causes people to respond to commercials and ads. Addictive behaviors are indiscriminate, while superfans are narrowly focused on a particular brand or product. Let's take my data as an example. Immersion data show that I am a superfan of the Guinness "Empty Chair" commercial, and I occasionally drink Guinness beer. But my superfandom is moderated by a desire for variety and the limited availability of Guinness on tap in California. Conversely, alcohol addicts will drink any kind of alcohol to satisfy their craving, even rubbing alcohol. Measuring neural responses does not brainwash people and create unbridled consumerism, a topic we will discuss in Chapter 7. It simply conveys to potential consumers information about a product or service in an effective and enjoyable way. Ultimately, the brain's prefrontal cortex integrates neural signals, including Immersion, into a decision. If one is not in the market for baby food, even the most immersive baby food commercial will not result in a purchase.

Since the body uses sugar as its primary fuel, it is not surprising that anticipation of a sugary sweet is highly immersive. Knowing this, some confectioners exaggerate anticipation to heighten the consumption experience. One that does is the Danish chocolatier Anthon Berg, which we will meet in Chapter 8 when we discuss the business of happiness. Anthon Berg's boxes are wrapped in cellophane and ribbon so one has to work to open them. The treats are also individually wrapped, building anticipation by slowing down consumption. The wrapping is crinkly and makes noise as the treat is revealed. Then the fatty mouthfeel of chocolate hits the tongue, initially suppressing the sweet taste. Each part of this process builds anticipation. The result: Danes consume an average of eleven pounds (4.9 kilograms) of chocolate per person every year, one of the highest rates in the world.

Marketers and sales associates should embrace anticipation as an effective strategy to sustain Immersion during advertising and product presentations. But there is a balance—present too slowly and people will be frustrated. Present too quickly and the power of anticipation is lost. We will explore the importance of anticipation further in the next chapter.

## BEER AND CHRISTMAS

People watch and rewatch commercials on video-sharing platforms, just like they watch other compelling narratives. The most-watched commercials include Apple's "1984," Wendy's "Where's the Beef?" Coca-Cola's "Meet Joe Greene," and Dos Equis's "Most Interesting Man in the World." But commercials are designed to influence purchases, not entertain. So why do people watch them repeatedly?

In 2006, Dos Equis was a niche beer brand produced by the Mexican brewery Cervecería Cuauhtémoc Moctezuma that only a select few knew about. When the "Most Interesting Man" commercials were launched, US sales of Dos Equis surged by 22% at a time when sales of imported beer fell 4%. Various incarnations of the commercials ran for twelve years and are still a hoot to watch. They inspired a meme, and *Saturday Night Live* even parodied them. The ads were so weird and fun that they created their own momentum, even among people who did not drink beer. The crazy adventures of this most interesting man just stuck in our heads.

Immersive stories—even commercials—can give us a jolt of joy. Even a small mood boost can raise one's satisfaction with life. Yes, you read that right: commercials can make you happier.

They also make TV better. Short, unexpected interruptions improve television viewing. Researchers at universities in California and New York found that US-style TV with a block of commercials every seven to eight minutes enhances the enjoyment of entertainment. This is true regardless of the quality of the commercials. Immersive experiences are metabolically costly and short breaks are an effective way to reset the brain to a lower Immersion level so the next experience can drive up Immersion. The brain values riding the rising wave of Immersion, not staying in some hyper-immersive state for long periods. At the same time, an Immersion peak while watching TV has a halo effect that sustains Immersion for at least the first commercial one views.

Some of the most memorable commercials are shown at Christmas and evoke feelings of nostalgia. During an interview for Headspace, journalist Diana Kelly asked me if nostalgia sells. It was a great question, so I ran a study to find out.

Neuroscientists have studied nostalgic music and found—no surprise—brain activation in regions associated with emotions and pleasure. Nostalgia also appears to improve people's moods, and people buy more when they are happier. Now you know why stores play familiar upbeat music. Diana's question was different: she asked if nostalgia was an effective advertising strategy.

My group collected Immersion data while people watched Christmas commercials for Target (Star Wars products), Hewlett-Packard (Sprocket mini-printer), Macy's (Thanksgiving Day parade), Amazon (Prime holiday shipping), and Campbell's Soup (building a snowman). As in nearly all of our advertising studies, self-reported measures—in this case, how nostalgic people felt—were unrelated to Immersion. Many Christmas ads feature children and pets, and these always juice self-reported "liking" measures. But these "cheats" seldom raise Immersion.

The neural data told a different story. The Campbell's Soup and Amazon commercials tied for the highest Immersion. Both companies' offerings were deftly integrated into the videos' narratives, generating solid product-story congruence. Going down the Immersion rankings, the Hewlett-Packard commercial wove a printer into a story moderately well and had average Immersion. HP's branding at the end occurred during a peak Immersion moment, increasing brand recall. The Target and Macy's commercials were a series of set pieces lacking a narrative. Each new scene produced a small Immersion peak as people oriented to them, but this was not enough to sustain Immersion. The commercials by Target and Macy's were more than two standard deviations below the advertising benchmark; they are unlikely to have any impact on sales.

Confirming our previous analyses, we found a positive relationship between the Immersion of nostalgic commercials and YouTube views. Nostalgia does appear to sell, but only if the product or service is woven into the story.

## A FORMULA

A Shiseido commercial for Waso facial wash that aired in Japan illustrates two neural mechanisms that drive market impact. The commercial starts by showing the product in its package, then the natural ingredients, and then a woman washing her face with the product. Then she smiles, just a little, showing us that she is enjoying this part of her daily routine.

Here's the neurobiology. The commercial opens with a white package of Waso displayed on a red platter, inducing the dopamine-driven attentional response due to the sharp color contrast. Dopamine is activated again by a cut to Waso's ingredients in a flowing tub. Fully 25% of the human brain is devoted to vision, and movement generates a larger response than does a static image. When the woman is first washing her face, her expression is neutral. Then she smiles subtly and viewers respond with oxytocin-driven emotional resonance. As empathic social creatures, we are happy because she is happy.

At this point, something really interesting happens in the brain. Oxytocin release induces another squirt of dopamine in a midbrain region called the striatum. This additional dopamine rewards us for acquiring social information; in this case, that face-washing can make one happy. The feedback loop from attention to social value to reward is the reason why commercials are enjoyable, memorable, and have market impact.

The in-house agency that created this commercial, Shiseido Creative, generated a neurologic triple whammy by adding in one more detail. As the woman is washing her face, the camera pans to the left side of her face. Just below her left eye, the model has a small dark mole. We see her smiling and washing her face, and our eyes are drawn to the mole. It's weird, and the brain fixates on weird because the unusual could be valuable. This induces another dopamine hit in the brain: the visual cortex identified something unexpected—woohoo! The striatal activation rewards us again for finding something unusual.

This beautiful commercial is nearly perfectly designed to generate high Immersion. The formula is: attention (dopamine) + movement (dopamine) + joy (oxytocin) + anomaly (dopamine). The Immersion data show that Immersion remains high for the full sixty seconds of the advertisement.

## WHY EMOTIONS MOVE MARKETS

The classic advertising model called AIDA was developed in 1898 by American ad man Elias St. Elmo Lewis. The acronym stands for Attention, Interest, Desire, and Action. St. Elmo Lewis wrote that "attention is to be concentrated and render every other portion of the ad display subordinate to that." Advertisers since then have privileged attention over the other three attributes. Attention is easily measured. It's the Nielsen box showing that a TV show is on, it is some proportion of newspaper or magazine subscribers to whom one can ascribe ad impressions, and it is a proportion of foot and car traffic going by billboards. In the age of the internet, attention has gotten even easier to measure: clicks, shares, and likes. Congratulations, your ad got attention. So, where are the sales?

Unfortunately, the data show attention is only very weakly associated with sales bumps from advertising. St. Elmo Lewis did not make the A model, but the AIDA model, and the other components do not automatically follow; they must be designed into advertising. Because measuring the other components is harder, agencies and analysts tend to avoid them. But neuroscientific studies show it is the full model that drives purchases.

Let's start with attention. You can think of attention as a binary variable: it is either zero or one. The term of art for this is *spot-light attention*. You can attend to A or B but not both. There is no multitasking, just rapid task switching because the attentional module in the brain is mostly binary ("mostly" because we are talking about conscious attention; the brain's unconscious attention is constantly scanning the environment—it is just that we are not aware of this). Conscious attention is associated with the neurotransmitter dopamine binding to receptors in the prefrontal cortex. Drugs for attention deficit disorder like Adderall are dopamine agonists that influence activity in the prefrontal cortex to increase attention.

Attention does not produce action on its own. For example, a brain imaging study that used dopaminergic activation to measure attention sought to predict song popularity but had an abysmal 30% accuracy. This is better than the 0% one gets using self-reported "liking," but one would still be better off flipping a coin. The published scientific research, from my lab and others, shows that attention is simply the necessary condition to motivate action, the last A in the AIDA model.

Attention opens the door to action, but the neurologic signature of emotional resonance causes people to act. Emotional resonance is nonbinary; it varies millisecond by millisecond, and when it reaches a crescendo, people take action. Emotion is what drives decisions.

Abandon hope all ye who pray to the false god Attention.

Go ahead and measure your clicks, but sales will not follow. Emotional resonance is the "Interest" component in the AIDA model and is the sufficient condition for people to take an action. Attention plus emotional resonance are therefore necessary and sufficient to influence behavior. When emotional resonance is sufficiently high, the brain is nudged out of homeostasis, its baseline state, and into decision mode.

Do high Immersion messages always move markets? While they often do, the message must be correctly targeted. The third part of the AIDA model is Desire. I have been calling this relevance. Without relevance, an immersive commercial can be pleasurable to the brain and may cause people to share it with others, but if desire is missing, then purchases will not follow.

Emotions can be measured, but this requires technology. Emotions are formed in evolutionarily old parts of the human brain that are largely outside of our conscious awareness, as we discussed in Chapter 1. Old-fashioned technologies like turning dials or so-called facial coding programs that claim to measure emotions fail scientific scrutiny. Emotions need to be measured where they are generated, in the evolutionarily old parts of the brain.

In 1898 Spain declared war on the United States, resulting in future president Teddy Roosevelt leading his Rough Riders into battle in Cuba. It was also the year Pierre and Marie Curie discovered radium and an ad man in Philadelphia developed a model to explain how his agency influenced purchases. It was only recently that the scientific foundations of the AIDA model were established, proving its value more than a century after its debut. Purchases can be influenced if a message or experience captures attention and, importantly, if it generates emotional resonance in a customer who desires the advertised product or service. Attention matters, but emotions are what move markets.

## RETURN ON IMMERSION

Reverse mortgages are loans that seniors take out against home equity to use for living expenses. The loan is repaid when seniors move or die. While Americans over the age of sixty-five are the fastest-growing demographic, the proportion of those living in homes with equity is small. This limits the ability of reverse mortgage companies to grow. But it does not stop them from trying.

A national reverse mortgage company hired an advertising agency to create TV commercials that would feature seniors living better because of reverse mortgage income. The agency measured Immersion while seniors watched rough cuts of several variants of commercials. They chose the most immersive roughs and edited them to increase Immersion. After several iterations, the commercials, backed by upbeat music from the 1950s and 1960s, were aired.

The reverse mortgage company had advertised on TV before and thus had a baseline for the expected number of website visits and phone calls the commercials would produce. The company reported to my group that the commercials edited for high Immersion generated a 30% uptick in requests for information about reverse mortgages. After being run on TV for six months, the videos were posted on YouTube and, as of this writing, have been seen by several hundred thousand people, extending the return on Immersion. The stories shown on these commercials do not need to immerse everyone, just the target audience who will find the information relevant to them.

## THE FUTURE OF STORYTELLING

I'm fairly sure Sailors' Snug Harbor is haunted.

Across Staten Island Sound from Lower Manhattan, for a century it was a haven for "aged, decrepit and worn-out" seamen until the cost to maintain the Greek Revival music halls, cottages, and chapels soared. The buildings themselves are now aged and decrepit but hauntingly beautiful. Even the spur off the Staten Island Railway that stopped at Sailors' Snug Harbor has been abandoned. The dank and humid grounds have witnessed murders, suicides, and forbidden relationships.

Publisher and multimedia storyteller Charlie Melcher invited me to Sailors' Snug Harbor for an event he created and curates called the Future of StoryTelling. The conference mixes storytellers with technologists to imagine new forms of entertainment. I scored an invitation after Melcher read media coverage of my analyses of a National Public Radio series called *StoryCorps*, in which people share personal anecdotes. Some of the *StoryCorps* narratives are extraordinary, like the tragedy of African American astronaut Ronald E. McNair, who was killed in the space shuttle *Challenger* explosion, as told by his brother. Others are so discursive that it is hard to follow them and even harder to find a point among all the chatter.

At the Future of StoryTelling, I discussed the convincing evidence my group had developed showing that a narrative arc is the most effective way to sustain Immersion. This story structure, first articulated in Aristotle's *Poetics* 2,300 years ago, starts with a mystery, builds tension with conflict, reaches a crisis, and then resolves it. A narrative arc immerses the lazy human brain in an unfolding human drama. We have tested whether stories with big stars or great music affect Immersion, but they make little difference. A narrative arc with authentic characters is really all it takes to be immersed.

What's the future of storytelling? Virtual reality (VR) and augmented reality (AR) will be part of the mix. A major social media company was preparing to launch an AR app and asked my team to help them evaluate neurologic responses to AR that promoted products. Average Immersion in AR commercials was 16% higher than the advertising benchmark, and the brands featured in AR apps got a 43% average lift in favorability ratings. The exception was AR experiences that did not have clear directions or had ambiguous goals. For these, frustration skyrocketed.

Neurologic responses to VR are similarly mixed. The data from a VR experience to support a movie franchise showed that VR is not uniformly more immersive than 2D movie trailers. Indeed, for many people VR experiences are frustrating because of missing "guides" or "guideposts" to draw users through variants of the story. For both AR and VR, using an Aristotelian story structure is the best way to create Immersion. Being part of a story creates a significant imprint on the brain, and if the story is structured well, it can be highly immersive.

Whether they are selling Tide or seeking donations to the Humane Society, my studies show that marketers have fifteen seconds to capture attention. After that, the mind wanders and Immersion is less likely to arise unless the narrative stokes emotions. Unlike our daily lives where we avoid tension, immersive stories create tension. As the characters work through conflict, we begin to see ourselves in the story and mimic their emotions. Shared emotions lead to shared actions. A call to action should ask people to do something right now, before immersive tension evaporates. This is precisely why marketers proclaim that "operators are standing by now."

Immersion in short-form content can happen in as quickly as three seconds. Creating immersive long-form experiences, like movies and TV shows, is an entirely different problem to which we turn next.

## KEY TAKEAWAYS

1. Advertisers have fifteen seconds to capture attention and then must provoke an emotional response.
2. Stories drive emotional attachment to products.
3. Extend peak emotional moments to improve branding recall.
4. Create peak Immersion at the end of messages to generate the biggest impact.
5. Effective commercials have product-story congruence.

# CHAPTER 3

# EXCEPTIONAL ENTERTAINMENT

"His scan showed severe dysfunction in the amygdala."

If you listen carefully when Dr. Curt Connors gives Peter Parker a tour of Oscorp early in the 2012 film *The Amazing Spider-Man*, you might catch me saying this. I was invited to create neuroscience dialogue on the Sony Pictures lot in Hollywood along with my friend, neuroscientist and filmmaker John Rubin.

Movies are filmed in layers. The first layer captures the movements and dialogue of the primary actors while bit players in the background pretend to talk but are actually silent. This is the best way to get clean audio from the actors who carry the movie. Later, in a process called automated dialogue replacement (ADR) or "looping," background dialogue is recorded and layered into the movie at just above whisper volume. *The*

*Amazing Spider-Man* had scenes in a neuroscience lab and, to the producers' credit, they wanted authentic ADR. I sat in a soundstage on the Sony Pictures lot with fifteen voice actors and a twenty-five-foot screen. The ADR director showed us a scene, assigned characters to the actors, and told us where to stand or sometimes walk relative to the microphones in the room. Then we had to create dialogue on the fly. The director described dialogue replacement as "seeing sausage being made" for movies. I recognized one of the voice actors as Kato Kaelin, famous for staying in O. J. Simpson's guest house the night Simpson's ex-wife Nicole was murdered; he seemed like a very nice guy when we chatted.

My visit to the Sony Pictures lot to improvise dialogue for *The Amazing Spider-Man* was the first time I had been on a movie lot. It only happened because of the one degree of separation rule: I live in Southern California, and when I spoke at TED Global in 2011 I became friends with Wendy Hoffman, who runs an ADR business in Hollywood. I have not started a new career as a voice actor, but I have worked with every major movie studio and many TV production companies to measure Immersion so they can create compelling entertainment.

This chapter will answer the following question: if humans have been entertaining each other for millennia, why don't creators of entertainment know good from bad while they are making it? Especially when serious money is on the line. We will start by diving into how movies are produced and marketed. Then we will move to other forms of entertainment—TV and music—to help us gain a fuller understanding of how entertainment can be improved by understanding what it does to the brain.

## THE RISK OF MOVIES

In 2002 Warner Bros. released an action/comedy/sci-fi movie called *The Adventures of Pluto Nash* starring Eddie Murphy. It cost $100 million to produce and earned $7 million, scoring an abysmal 4% on the review aggregator Rotten Tomatoes. In 2002 Columbia Pictures released the Jennifer Lopez and Ben Affleck bomb *Gigli*, which cost $75 million to make and earned a paltry $7 million. Its Rotten Tomatoes rating is 6%. The economic risk movie studios and distributors face is enormous: in 2017 Sony Pictures lost $1 billion.

Studios attempt to manage risk using data. Rough cuts of movies are screened for test audiences, and the state of the art is to—wait for it—distribute pencils and index cards and ask people what they liked. Did you like the ending? Were you sad when the dog died? The perceived wisdom by at least some studio executives is that these comments are actually useful. If so, what happened with *Pluto Nash* and *Gigli*?

The marketing of movies is more straightforward than production, so let's start there. The cost to market a major motion picture is typically half of what is spent to produce it. *Pluto Nash*'s $100 million production budget demanded that distributor Warner Bros. spend $50 million to receive a return on money paid to the movie production companies, Castle Rock Entertainment and Village Roadshow Pictures. Marketing costs vary substantially depending on the type of movie, its target demographic, the actors in it, and even the time of year the movie is released. The most expensive movie produced to date is 2011's *Pirates of the Caribbean: On Stranger Tides,* which cost close to $400 million. Marketing costs were estimated at $150 million and included a commercial shown during the 2011 Super Bowl, a 3D theatrical trailer, a video game, a phone app, and even jewelry. Marketing budgets for high-profile films can top 100% of the production costs. Movie distributors spent approximately $4 billion on marketing worldwide in 2020.

Movie ticket sales are notoriously difficult to predict. Actually, studios really only care about the first couple of weeks of movie ticket sales. Revenue sharing between theater owners and the companies that distribute movies work on a sliding scale in which distributors earn the highest percentage in the first week, often 70–90% of ticket sales, and may earn as little as 30% at the end of the run.

The amount of money movie distributors have at risk means that they are obsessed with creating movie trailers that put butts in theater seats. Studios hire trailer production specialists who develop multiple trailers per movie. Some will be shown in theaters domestically, others internationally, some will play on TV, and some will be released online. The audiences' reactions to the first trailers released affect the editing of subsequent trailers. Sometimes edits to trailers are made just days before a movie is released.

This is a high-stakes game, and the studios tweak and pivot to try to convince a few additional tenths of a percent of the population to buy tickets. My team and I wondered if Immersion in movie trailers could predict movie ticket sales. Since this would be a challenge, we started small.

## SMALL-SCALE PREDICTIONS

Our first study used Immersion data from the Facebook small-screen study we discussed in Chapter 2. We limited our investigation to *The Fault in Our Stars* and *Get Hard*. These movies were produced for $12 million and $40 million, respectively, and were targeted at quite different audiences. We did not test the *Entourage* trailer because it was awful and we thought it would bias our analysis.

For the time being, we ignored non-neurologic factors that affect box office receipts and focused on how accurately Immersion alone would predict revenue. Participants were asked if they enjoyed the trailer, if they thought it was entertaining, and if they would share it with friends. These impressions, as in our previous research, did not predict box office receipts. More to the point, the *Get Hard* trailer was higher on all "liking" measures than *The Fault in Our Stars*, yet *The Fault in Our Stars'* opening week was 35% higher than the opening for *Get Hard*. In contrast to self-report responses, Immersion showed a positive relationship with box office receipts. The trailer for *The Fault in Our Stars* generated 41% higher Immersion than the trailer for *Get Hard*, nearly matching the difference in first-week ticket sales.

Our small-scale test encouraged us to do a larger study to see if Immersion in movie trailers might predict ticket sales beyond the two trailers we tested. Honestly, I was quite skeptical we would find anything. Data analysts working for movie distributors have built sophisticated statistical models that use economic and demographic variables to predict ticket sales. We had successfully predicted the market impact of advertising, but movie trailers are a different beast, and my team and

I could not be sure that the same techniques would continue to work. Even something as simple as the length of theatrical trailers—typically three minutes, versus thirty or sixty seconds for commercials—could throw off the entire approach.

In our next study, we scaled up our analysis to nine movies of varying quality, including one movie that had not yet been released. The unreleased movie would be our "out-of-sample" prediction based on the model we built from the released movies. We recruited forty-nine adults aged eighteen to seventy to watch trailers for some of the best and worst movies, along with current releases. This gave us a solid spread in the data. The trailers were *47 Ronin, American Hustle, Birdman, Her, Inherent Vice, Dawn of the Planet of the Apes, The Hundred-Foot Journey, The Master,* and *Transformers: Age of Extinction.* The 2013 Keanu Reeves movie *47 Ronin* is one of the biggest box office bombs; its $175 million production budget nearly bankrupted Universal Studios. On the other end of the spectrum, *Transformers: Age of Extinction* earned over $1 billion against a $210 million production budget. *Birdman,* a movie that would eventually win four Academy Awards, including Best Picture, opened under $3 million. The Joaquin Phoenix film *Inherent Vice* had not been released when we did our analysis; we would generate a prediction of its box office and wait to see how accurate our prediction was.

Just as in our small-scale study, the reported likability of the movie trailer did not predict revenue at the box office. In contrast, Immersion alone predicted 25% of the variation in first-week revenue. Immersion, that unusual neurologic combination of attention and emotional resonance, seems to capture the value the brain places on an experience. Importantly for this small sample of eight movies, Immersion correctly classified movies as having high or low ticket sales with 61% accuracy. That information alone can guide distributors on how much they should invest in marketing a movie.

So what else predicts ticket sales? We looked at two dozen economic and creative variables, including the "star power" of the actors (a measure developed by the Internet Movie Database [IMDb] based on ticket sales of movies in which an actor has appeared), the director's power ranking (another IMDb measure), genre, the number of views of the Wikipedia page about the movie, whether the movie was a sequel, and the production budget. The strongest predictor of ticket sales is a movie's budget: it explains 36% of first-week ticket sales. Movies with bigger budgets have bigger stars, more special effects, longer shoot times, and may be filmed in exotic locations. Following the 50% rule, they also tend to have larger marketing budgets.

Even after including all these factors, Immersion adds predictive power to traditional statistical models of ticket sales. Besides measuring what the brain values, Immersion is statistically unrelated to a movie's budget and other variables. Fresh variables improve forecasts. For the eight movies in our mini-study, Immersion increased predictive accuracy by nine percentage points. Better accuracy means better budgeting for marketing and more money made. Nine percentage points may sound modest, but movie marketers consider a one-tenth of a percent change important because of the millions of people who are potential audience members.

We used the statistical model we had built for the eight movies to generate a box office forecast for movie nine, *Inherent Vice*, before it was released. The model included average Immersion while people watched the trailer for *Inherent Vice*, the movie's $20 million production budget, and a January indicator variable. *Inherent Vice*'s broad opening was January 9, 2015. January is a typical "dump" month for movies that are not expected to resonate with the public. Patrons are assumed to be fatigued from watching Christmas releases and watching family members bicker. The model predicted first-week ticket sales of $7 million. *Inherent Vice*'s actual ticket sales for the week ending January 15 were $5.3 million. We were off, but not by that much. Immersion improved the accuracy of this out-of-sample prediction by 14% over standard economic variables. This is a substantial improvement over the standard models movie distributors use.

## HIGH-IMPACT MOVIE TRAILERS

Next task: scale up to discover why some trailers effectively drive ticket sales. We confirmed the predictive accuracy of Immersion by measuring neural responses to forty-four movie trailers. The trailers were as varied as *Justin Bieber: Never Say Never, Car 54: Where Are You?* And *The Crying Game*. Neurologic variables alone identified box office hits versus bombs with 78% accuracy. Moreover, ticket sales increased linearly with people's Immersion in the movie trailer; the data showed a positive correlation of 0.30 between Immersion and box office. In this larger study, Immersion added 25% predictive ability above the movie's economic and creative variables. More data produced better predictions.

After we measured Immersion for several hundred movie

trailers, the data showed that winning trailers had several distinct elements. An effective movie trailer must open "hot," with characters immediately facing a mystery or crisis. In a typical narrative, the crisis would resolve as the story ends. Instead, movie trailers that put butts in seats stop at the point of highest tension, leaving the story unresolved. One must purchase a ticket to see how the characters get through the crisis.

In addition, movie touchstones and iconography should be liberally spread throughout the trailer. Placing these at peak Immersion points will increase their association with the movie and reignite interest when used in collateral advertising. *The Amazing Spider-Man* trailer does this by repeatedly showing spiders, spiderwebs, and Peter Parker in his red and blue suit. As with commercials, the date of release and movie title should be shown during an Immersion peak. Nearly all trailers put this crucial information at the end when Immersion is typically low. My analysis shows that trailer producers should break the mold and include the release date and movie title in several places in a typical three-minute trailer. This reinforces the call to action since many people tune out or click away after a few seconds of content.

## EDITING FOR IMPACT

Several major movie studios currently measure Immersion to evaluate different versions of movie trailers. This means I occasionally return to movie lots to watch trailers evolve. One hot summer day, I watched the team at Paramount Pictures measuring rough cuts of trailers for their Christmas releases. These included two "tent-pole" movies that would make or break annual profitability. In order to quickly identify where to put their efforts, Paramount's team invited several dozen people from their accounting and finance departments to a large conference room and handed out smartwatches with the Immersion app.

One of the trailers they spent serious time on was the sixth installment in a sci-fi franchise. It cost over $100 million to make, and the Paramount team tested low-resolution versions of three trailers for it. The most immersive trailer was within 1% of the median Immersion benchmark for advertising, indicating that it was good. But it could be better. The marketing staff and the movie's producer worked with the trailer producer to increase the trailer's Immersion prior to release, ultimately raising it 18% over the tested rough. Peak Immersion for the theatrical trailer increased more than 100% compared to the rough that was first tested.

Paramount's team made four changes to raise Immersion. First, they built a stronger narrative arc that built tension as soon as the characters were introduced. Second, they put more focus on the human protagonist and the emotions she feels, and less focus on the nonhuman creatures. Third, they added more close-ups of faces of the humans and the creatures. Finally, they ended the trailer with high tension by showing the human protagonist in danger.

The result? Production costs were covered by day seven of the movie's release while competing against a movie starring Jason Momoa and another one with Emily Blunt. The stellar revenue performance was due, in part, to the improved theatrical trailer.

It is much easier to diagnose how to improve trailers when you have data. An enormous amount of work goes into making these mini-dramas. People will only leave the house and go to one of the forty thousand movie theaters in the US if distributors can produce trailers that shake up viewers' brains.

## GOING LONG

Once we had a handle on three-minute movie trailers, we decided to see if Immersion could identify why full-length movies are hits. Again, we started small. I asked members of my team to watch a movie in a nearby theater while wearing smartwatches. I randomly picked *The Hitman's Bodyguard* starring Ryan Reynolds and Samuel L. Jackson. The movie ran 118 minutes, and Immersion averaged across participants and across the entire movie was...average. This movie would earn $177 million against a $30 million production budget. With such a large return on investment, how could it be average?

To answer this question, we need a bit more neuroscience. Remember that Immersion is normalized to vary from zero to one hundred, but unlike self-reported "liking" of an experience where people may give a movie a one hundred, Immersion averaged across participants will be much closer to its average of around fifty (the actual average varies by the type of experience). This happens for two reasons.

First, as we discussed in Chapter 2, human brains crave homeostasis, or a condition of balance. Because of this, brains cannot sustain a deeply immersive state for more than thirty to forty seconds. You can think about hitting Immersion of one hundred as maxing out your brain's processing capacity. After that, neurons fatigue and Immersion drops as brain resources must be devoted to other tasks. This is exactly why movie theaters are dark and compel people not to talk. This frees up neural bandwidth for deep Immersion.

The second reason that Immersion for long events like movies tends to be near the average is that a typical measurement of twenty people averages their neural states at each time point. Even though brains work similarly, they don't work perfectly in sync. So, if person X's brain is highly immersed in an experience and hits a one hundred for a few seconds, person Y's brain might reach an eighty-five or ninety a second or two later. Due to averaging, aggregate neural responses almost never reach zero or one hundred. Next, second-by-second responses are averaged over an entire experience. This effect is less severe for short-form content like commercials and movie trailers but really kicks in for experiences that last an hour or more.

Neural fatigue and averaging always produce a wavy pattern for Immersion. When we pull apart the components of Immersion to examine the contributions of attention and emotional resonance to the wavy pattern, most of the variation is due to emotion. As we discussed in Chapter 2, attention is a binary response; one is either paying attention or not. As a result, variations in emotional resonance drive the second-by-second variation in Immersion. This means that Immersion peaks are moments of high emotion—just the reason I created this measure.

What about the emotional low points of an experience? I created another measure, which I have called "frustration," that identifies when people are paying attention but are emotionally disengaged. In other words, their brains do not value the experience they are having at that moment. Frustration adds up the valleys as Immersion evolves over time. By collecting data on thousands of people in a variety of experiences, I have calculated norms for average Immersion, peak Immersion, and frustration. When creators edit content to increase peak Immersion or reduce frustration, they drive up average Immersion, increasing the impact of their output.

We can dig into *The Hitman's Bodyguard* using all three measures to understand why it performed so well at the box office. Average Immersion for the movie was within a couple percentage points of the benchmark for long-form entertainment. Peak Immersion was even better, 13% higher than the entertainment benchmark. It won't spoil the movie if I tell you that the seemingly unkillable bad guy is killed at the end, resolving the tension in the story. This scene, shown during the last minute of the movie, was twice as immersive compared to the five minutes before it. Because the movie activates the peak-end rule, audiences remember it as highly enjoyable.

The data also showed that the high points of the movie were diminished by abundant frustration. Frustration was 24% higher than the entertainment benchmark indicating that people were "checked out" for chunks of the movie.

Measuring Immersion during the movie's editing could have improved its already strong box office. Modifying the story to make the peaks higher and longer would have raised Immersion. At the same time, cutting out the frustration points would have kept people immersed throughout the movie. Yet every story needs peaks and valleys. Let's find out why.

## GOING LONGER

Long stories have specific structures that exploit the wavy pattern of Immersion. I'll explain the neuroscience of long-form stories by continuing to analyze *The Hitman's Bodyguard*. The movie has three primary storylines: the bodyguard has to get the hitman to a tribunal without allowing him to get killed by mobsters; the hitman and bodyguard are sworn enemies and have to figure out how to work together; and the hitman is deeply in love with his wife and must survive testifying to see her again. The three plotlines are woven together through the film. Storytellers have realized since time immemorial that high Immersion for long periods exhausts people. Filmmakers and novelists work around this neurologic constraint by using multiple storylines.

As one storyline drives up Immersion, the film switches to a different storyline that has lower tension. This gives viewers a neurologic breather while still moving the narrative forward. As Immersion in the second storyline increases, a third storyline can be introduced with initially lower Immersion, drawing on fewer neural resources. Introducing new storylines requires that the audience pay attention to follow the changes. The writers must build in hooks so that the audience is emotionally involved in each storyline. Neurologically, this requires that information is kept in working memory.

In *The Hitman's Bodyguard*, the highest Immersion peak occurs when the antagonist, who is trying to kill the hitman, finally gets his chance. The hitman and the bodyguard, who are enemies, must ultimately cooperate to stop the killer. This scene resolves two of the three storylines. The movie does not need to resolve the last storyline—reuniting the hitman with his beloved wife—because we can anticipate that this will happen because he has survived.

Just because long-form entertainment hits the average for Immersion does not mean it will be unsuccessful. For example, 25% of *The Hitman's Bodyguard*'s viewers were superfans in our mini-study. Superfans are vitally important because they watch a movie two or three times and tell others they should see it. Identifying demographic segments who are superfans shows movie distributors who will spread the word about movies they love. Often, the data shows that superfans are quite different than moviemakers expect. This is valuable intelligence that distributors can exploit to promote their movies. Movie distributors can identify superfans in online forums, or by putting displays in movie theaters trading tchotchkes for contact information, or through free app downloads with movie outtakes and commentary. Collecting this information before a movie's release and in the first week of release can put "legs" into a movie's run.

## THE VALUE OF SUPERFANS

All the major movie studios have departments that create opportunities for superfans to continuously engage with content from their favorite TV shows and movie franchises. From writing fan fiction to attending Comic-Con and *Star Trek* conventions, superfans spend time and money to promote entertainment properties. Identifying attributes of superfans when they view content enables entertainment distributors to engage them immediately without waiting to see who shows up at the Marvel booth at Comic-Con. Superfans can even be found before a program is released.

A major unscripted TV production company measured Immersion while people watched a sizzle reel for a show the company would pitch to a cable network. The true crime program they were measuring featured a private detective who found missing persons when the police could not. The producers told me that they knew that the core audience for this genre was women.

Interviewing women in the study confirmed their interest in the show. When I spoke to the men in the focus group, only half of them said they would watch the series. But the Immersion data told another story: 25% of the superfans were men. Interestingly, when the men in the room were told that their brains liked the show, they changed their statements and said that, actually, they would watch it. This demonstrates the malleability of self-reported data.

There are a number of ways the production company could create value from knowing the show had male superfans. First, the show could be sold to a general interest network rather than a more female-focused outlet. A larger audience increases how much the producers earn from the show. Second, the producers had hundreds of hours of film of the detective. They could create a second show that included additional aspects that would appeal to men. For example, the second show could spend more time on the technology used to find bodies and the weapons the detective carries during his work. The producers could then sell two shows, one more female-oriented and the other targeted toward men.

Unexpected superfans are golden nuggets from which production companies and distributors can profit. I attended an Immersion measurement at a major movie studio when their staff tested movie trailers for a comedy featuring African American women. The data showed that most superfans were women of color, but 20% of middle-aged white men who watched the trailer were superfans. A marketing plan for this niche demographic could drive up ticket sales. This "neurographic" profile complements psychographic and demographic profiles that marketers use when micro-targeting online ad placement.

This process can be reversed by finding the character in a film or TV show who resonates most strongly with an audience and building a marketing campaign around him or her. My friend Chris Gebhardt produced a documentary called *Unlikely* featuring Americans struggling to get a college education. My team helped Chris measure Immersion during a pre-release screening of the film. As expected, Immersion averaged across attendees and over the entire movie was near the entertainment benchmark. Examining the second-by-second data, we found the highest Immersion peaks occurred when a twenty-nine-year-old African American woman named Clarissa was featured. Clarissa woke up at 4:00 a.m. to get her children ready for school so she could attend classes at the University of Akron. Peak Immersion indicated that the audience had formed an emotional connection to Clarissa. The data convinced Gebhardt's team to edit the film's conclusion so it featured Clarissa. They also built the marketing campaign for the movie around this amazing woman. Here's the takeaway: superfans (and everyone else) need a super-character to care about.

## SCRIPTS

A typical Hollywood script reader will power through ten to fifteen film treatments or TV scripts a week. If they find something with potential, they'll write a "coverage" or synopsis of the story and comment on its strengths and weaknesses. The coverage will be sent to a studio or creative agency executive for review. The executive may decide to read the script or book a meeting with the writer. Before a script is sent to a studio, aspiring screenwriters can, for a fee, have a professional script reader evaluate their work to improve it. Among the places to get feedback on a script is a website called The Black List.

Franklin Leonard, a dynamic Harvard-trained writer and movie development executive at Leonardo DiCaprio's production company, Appian Way, was frustrated by how many good scripts he read that were not made into movies. Almost on a lark, in 2005 he created a spreadsheet with the titles of what he thought were the year's best unproduced scripts and sent this to seventy-five producers he knew, asking for quality ratings since everyone reads the same scripts. He called this The Black List.

In essence, Leonard was crowdsourcing script evaluation, and the idea took off. The spreadsheet evolved into a website that has hosted over one thousand screenplays. Roughly a third of them have been produced, including acclaimed and successful films such as *Argo, American Hustle, Juno, The King's Speech, Slumdog Millionaire,* and *The Revenant.* Writers pay a monthly fee to post their scripts on The Black List and have coverages written by professionals. Producers and their staff read the coverages and can contact writers for meetings or to make purchase offers. Scripts are registered at the Writers Guild of America or similar organizations before they are shopped around to reduce the theft of intellectual property.

In 2017, Leonard visited my lab to see our technology in action. One difficulty with script evaluation is that there is no specific training that qualifies one as a script expert. If the script reader thinks the script is a dud, into the garbage it goes. An additional problem is that scripts from different movie genres are not easily comparable to each other. One of my favorite movies is Christopher Nolan's *Memento*, starring Guy Pearce. I like it for many reasons, but especially because Nolan accurately captures the behavioral aberrations of patients who are unable to form long-term memories. One of the best things about *Memento* (spoiler alert) is that its timeline runs partially backward; not backward linearly, but backward, forward, and backward. The brilliance of Nolan's script is that the narrative arc is also an arc when one goes in reverse. How can the script for *Memento* be compared to nearly every other script that has time moving forward? Franklin Leonard asked me if neuroscience could complement the opinions of script readers.

The Black List has produced "table reads" of scripts on its website. During a table read, actors recite the script in character, expressing emotions that are necessary for listeners to be immersed in the story. Emotional expression is blunted when one reads to oneself. I randomly chose a recorded table read from The Black List called *Maggie's Dawn* to see what we could learn by measuring neural responses. The script was written by Blaine Tyler and depicts a post-apocalyptic survival-of-the-strongest world with sentient robots doing the bidding of humans—at least for a while.

I measured Immersion while eight people listened to the table read. Average Immersion for the script was 38.6, a bit below the benchmark of 46 for long-form entertainment. Peak Immersion and frustration were also near their entertainment benchmarks. The best way to use brain responses when assessing scripts is to evaluate the impact of specific scenes and identify areas that need rewrites. The data showed that Immersion rose strongly when the protagonists were talking and surged at the screenplay's climax. This shows that the audience is emotionally connecting to the characters.

The data indicated that *Maggie's Dawn* was good enough to be produced. The story maintained an effective balance between the familiar hero's journey and an unexpected world with hard-to-predict twists. The main characters' personalities were revealed in small chunks as the story evolved, giving the audience a reason to emotionally connect to them. *Maggie's Dawn* did have half a dozen scenes in which Immersion tanked. These could be punched up to improve the movie's box office and reduce the risk of producing a flop. As of this writing, the script is in development at an independent production company.

Science is starting to invade script evaluation. A host of companies use artificial intelligence to analyze the content of scripts using past successes and failures to train their algorithms. Soon, computer algorithms will write scripts themselves. Artificial intelligence is necessarily backward-looking since it has to be trained. This may lead to the homogenization of movies. The neuroscience approach to script evaluation is forward-looking and objectively determines whether a scene has the impact the filmmaker wants it to have. Remember from Chapter 2 that the brain loves things that are unusual. While it can be difficult for artificial intelligence to find outliers, the brain always responds to a new thing. As in *Maggie's Dawn*, story novelty must be balanced with contextual familiarity. The brain loves the new, but not too new. Rather than having one or a few people determine if a movie should be made, the Creative+ approach measures Immersion or some other brain response during script evaluation to uncover unexpected hits.

## UNSCRIPTED TV

Fully one half of the 400 highest-rated television shows in 2020 were unscripted. There is a good reason for this: they are cheap to produce. Avoiding big salaries for big stars means less up-front cost and a reduced risk of financial loss if the show fails to find an audience. By 2021, the number of people watching the major US TV networks had fallen by nearly two-thirds compared to the broadcast TV peak in the late 1990s. A smaller audience jeopardizes advertising revenue for the major networks and cable channels and increases the risk that higher-cost scripted shows will lose money.

Unscripted TV shows can turn a profit if they capture even modest audiences, typically on cable channels. These shows run the gamut from ratings darlings *Survivor* and *America's Got Talent* to disappointments like *Comfort Food Tour* and *Flipping Virgins*. Cable channels can purchase these shows on the cheap, at least initially, before they prove they can attract an audience. Think *MythBusters*. At the same time, distributors sometimes overpay for new shows that barely register in the ratings because, for example, they feature a well-known star. The inability to predict ratings for unscripted shows creates market inefficiencies, hurting both production companies and TV networks.

Dorsey Pictures, a midsize reality TV production company, challenged us to predict the ratings of unscripted TV shows. I warned CEO Chris Dorsey that this may be asking more of neuroscience than it was capable of delivering. A variety of factors besides the quality of the content affect ratings, including the time and day the show is aired, competing content, advertising, the penetration of DVR ownership by the show's target demographic, and even the weather. My team was not even sure how much TV content we would have to evaluate to predict ratings.

Here's what we decided to do: Dorsey Pictures picked top- and bottom-rated unscripted shows from six major US cable channels, twenty-five shows in all. They identified the target demographic for these shows, and we recruited eighty-four people who fit this profile and paid them to watch content. But how much content?

All human experiments face two constraints: fatigue and bladder capacity. Watching twenty-five shows, each with twenty-two minutes of content, would keep participants trapped in my lab for more than nine hours. Not only is this infeasible, but fatigue degrades data quality. Instead, we decided to see if showing people the first act of shows (eight to ten minutes) would be enough to predict ratings winners. We also included short breaks to let participants rest their brains and empty their bladders.

Even this pared-down approach generated over half a million

seconds of neurologic data. Immersion for each show was averaged across viewers, and then we estimated a standard statistical model to see how accurately the data could distinguish the ten top-rated shows from the fifteen with low ratings. Self-reported data on people's stated intentions to watch a show predicted hits with a pitiful 17% accuracy. All other self-reported data, such as "liking" a show, were even less accurate. The neural data did much better. A show's average Immersion and average frustration identified top-rated shows with 84% accuracy. When we included whether participants had seen the show before, predictive accuracy increased to 88%. As a double check, we added to the model self-reported data on "liking" and "intend to watch." These variables did not improve the predictive accuracy at all.

Chris Dorsey's team was blown away when they saw that neurologic data could nearly perfectly predict ratings. He told me that the predictions from TV networks are no better than flipping a coin. The market inefficiency when buying new shows could be resolved by measuring brain responses. Then ratings could be objectively predicted and a fair price set.

I decided to see how far I could push the neural data by asking: how soon would the brain know a good show? We used the first minute of each show to calculate average Immersion and frustration and then estimated the same statistical model. These truncated data still predicted which shows were hits with 80% accuracy. We had only lost four percentage points of accuracy by throwing away 90% of the data. Not only does the brain recognize a good story, but it does so rapidly. Script evaluators should use this approach. Rather than read the entire script, or most of it, they can measure neural responses to the first ten minutes of a table read to get a quick indicator of the story's potential.

The data provided insights into success in the reality TV world. Top-rated unscripted shows immediately introduce a crisis or mystery and build Immersion as the show's participants are introduced. Unlike scripted shows that create emotional attachment to characters over multiple episodes in a season, unscripted TV shows have to get audiences to care about on-screen characters rapidly because they may appear in only one episode. This is done by focusing on one or two key characters who audiences get to know. One of the superstars of the unscripted world, producer Maz Farrelly, who brought *Big Brother*, *Dancing with the Stars*, *The X Factor*, and *Celebrity Apprentice* to life, told me that ensemble shows are built around a single person. The person at the center, the "glue," must be the same on camera and off, fully comfortable in his or her skin. If not, viewers quickly recognize that the person is playing a part and will not emotionally engage. Without an emotional connection, there is little reason to keep watching. Once the glue is identified, the peak emotional moments of a season are cataloged and the season is built with a storyline for each episode. Many unscripted shows build in challenges and conflict to see how people respond. This requires that participants are shown in a consistent way in each episode and that tension points are foreshadowed. In shows in which people are voted off, producers must also plant expectations about who might win.

Unscripted TV will continue to grow due to its low cost and the plethora of narrow target audiences on cable channels and streaming services. Shows like *Who's Your Daddy?*—which made a game out of a woman's attempt to find her real father—

and *Farmer Wants a Wife* are not going away. Unfortunately, the use of competition to build tension is overused. Why are the world's best chefs hamstrung with limited ingredients and a countdown clock in shows *Iron Chef America* and *Chopped*? The data show that story trumps artificial tension.

## SYNDICATION

The top-rated US TV show in the 1990s was the extraordinarily well-written *Seinfeld*. A twenty-two minute episode had three to four storylines that intersected in the show's ending. The writers of *Seinfeld* exploited the brain's preferred wavy pattern of Immersion by varying tension across different storylines and providing the relief of a laugh. This "show about nothing" was stealthily about something: the absurdity of everyday life. *Seinfeld* is shown daily on cable channels and streams on Netflix. Nearly everyone born in 1980 or earlier has seen *Seinfeld*. But with so much new content available, why are people still watching old shows?

The traditional syndication threshold for broadcast TV was that at least one hundred episodes of a series had to air to ensure profitability. This milestone kept shows like *Rules of Engagement*, starring David Spade, and *Ghost Whisperer*, starring Jennifer Love Hewitt, alive until they hit the magical hundredth. Today, with multiple narrowcast opportunities, even a single-season show like 2002's *Firefly*, or my COVID-lockdown favorite, *Counterpart*, which ran for twenty episodes, have active post-broadcast lives. TV and movie distributors like Paramount, Sony, and Warner Bros. generate significant revenue by selling syndication rights to cable networks and online portals like Hulu and Amazon.

In 2018, Warner Bros. Television asked us to help them identify the neural attraction of syndicated shows. The research department at Warner Bros. measured Immersion while eighty-seven people watched ninety-second clips of twenty-four shows in syndication. The study included recent shows being syndicated for the first time, such as *Black Mirror* and *The Handmaid's Tale*, and a number of syndication stalwarts including *The Simpsons*, *Golden Girls*, and *Brooklyn Nine-Nine*.

The data established that the brain values familiar TV programs more than unfamiliar ones. We had previously shown that immersive stories continue to immerse people when they hear or watch them again, but my team and I were surprised to find in this study that Immersion *increased* during additional viewings. The reason? Peak Immersion in familiar shows was 38% higher than it was for unfamiliar shows. This was not because older shows have better stories. The second-by-second data revealed Immersion peaks when viewers saw their favorite characters. These data show that viewers had formed emotional attachments to characters they knew well. We built a statistical model to see if neural data alone could identify which shows people had seen before. The model was able to predict this with 76% accuracy.

Emotional connections to our "TV friends" make syndication profitable. Rather than breeding contempt, familiarity breeds Immersion. Distributors have discovered that the one-hundred-episode rule was too conservative. The social brain forms attachments rapidly, driving up Immersion when social experiences are wrapped in a story. When I measured my own Immersion while watching *Counterpart* a second time, I had an Immersion spike when the protagonist, played by JK

Simmons, was on screen. After finishing *Counterpart*, I was craving more JK Simmons and started searching for other shows and movies he was in. Syndicators should consider buying the rights to the catalog of output from programs in which actors generate Immersion spikes in order to monetize the brain's blunt attachment system. More generally, businesses of all types should tap into the brain's attachment to people and rituals as foundations for customer loyalty. We will examine how this is done in Chapter 5.

## MOVED BY MUSIC

No data needed: he was immersed. But he would not follow my directions.

Lightning in a Bottle is an annual outdoor music festival, art installation, and social experience. Years ago, when we measured the neurochemical constituents of Immersion with blood draws, we obtained permission to measure the social effect of music when thousands of people were together. During the after-event blood draw, one participant was so moved that he was sobbing and wanted a hug. After the blood draw I told him; for now he had to sit still so I could find a vein. Our data showed that music caused a surge in oxytocin and that this effect was stronger when people had an experience together.

Music's key, tempo, meter, and words combine to produce identifiable brain responses. Memories flood in and emotions flood out. Minor keys are associated with negative emotions like sadness and anxiety, while major keys signal joy and love. Producers of movies, TV shows, and commercials have put considerable effort into choosing the right music ever since the silent era when organists played live. Music is still understood to be important, since hiring leading composers like John Williams or Hans Zimmer to write a musical score will set a production back millions of dollars. Other films license well-known songs. Martin Scorsese used the Rolling Stones' "Gimme Shelter" when showing mob violence in *Casino*, and Francis Ford Coppola used The Doors' "The End" during the opening sequence of *Apocalypse Now*. Both songs reminded viewers of the eras these movies were set in.

But just how much does music matter? Some superb movies have little or no music. The 2008 Joel and Ethan Coen movie *No Country for Old Men* had sound, but no musical score. It won four Academy Awards, including Best Picture, proving that movies without music can have powerful effects on audiences. Whether music matters in movies seemed like something my team should test.

We asked twenty participants to watch a forty-second scene of Captain Jack Sparrow alone in a boat from one of the *Pirates of the Caribbean* movies while we measured Immersion. The original scene had triumphal music, and a YouTuber had overlaid different musical scores on the scene, seeking to evoke different emotions. The new music was identified as "scary and foreboding," "comical," and "sad and thoughtful." We also showed the clip without music.

Changing the music caused Immersion for the scene to vary by 30%. The highest Immersion occurred for sad and thoughtful music, and the lowest for scary music. Immersion for the original triumphal score was right in the middle. Compared to the scene without music, Immersion peaks were higher and more sustained with music. In fact, music doubled the number of neurologic superfans for the clip compared to the silent version. The neuroscience confirms the conventional wisdom that the music in a scene should accentuate the emotions the audience is meant to feel. While the Coen brothers are movie-making iconoclasts who often skip the music, most directors should use music to increase Immersion in the narrative.

But another problem crops up. If music supervisors want to use existing music in the soundtrack, they have an almost infinite number of songs from which to choose. Indeed, consumers face the same problem when curating their own playlists. Here's the data: every day twenty-four thousand new songs are released worldwide. Every day. That translates into 8.7 million new songs every year. People are drowning in choices, and music distributors have an increasingly difficult time identifying which songs might be hits. Producers' inability to predict hits means that artists are often underpaid for their work, and music labels misallocate their marketing budgets when seeking to build audiences for new music.

A Los Angeles startup company, Steereo, exposes rideshare patrons to music before it is released. The Steereo platform monitors the music riders listen to and for how long to tell music distributors which songs have found an audience. Steereo's CEO, Anne Kavanagh, asked us if we could also use brain responses to identify songs that would become hits.

The typical rider listens to a Steereo song for about one minute, and we wanted to replicate this effect in our study. I was not sure how effectively Immersion would predict hit music, so I suggested we start small. Kavanagh picked seven unreleased songs from Steereo's Artists in Residence Program. My team measured Immersion while twenty-one people listened to the first minute of each song. Listeners were also asked to rate how much they "liked" each song. The songs were released a month after we measured Immersion so there was no way to rig the data to improve the results. Steereo shared several measures of song popularity with us to see how many we could forecast.

Immersion almost perfectly predicted the number of Spotify streams one month after a song's release (correlation: 0.92). Conversely, listeners' "liking" of a song had no ability to predict Spotify streams. Immersion was highly correlated with other measures of song popularity, including song completions by Steereo rideshare listeners and Shazam lookups. For example, Immersion predicted song completions by Steereo listeners with 71% accuracy. Neural responses to songs can also be a marketing guide: the number of neurologic superfans predicted an artist's Spotify followers with 67% accuracy. These types of data can be used by music distributors to build a demographic profile of superfans in order to build an enthusiastic audience and create a hit.

New hit songs are generally similar to previous hits but just different enough to capture dopaminergic attention. When the lyrics and music generate emotional resonance, Immersion kicks in. The "same but new" principle applies not only to music, but also to lyrics. Finding a fresh angle on topics thousands of songs have covered—attraction, love, heartache—requires the songwriter to balance the familiar and the novel. An example is the hauntingly beautiful 2017 song

"If We Were Vampires" by Jason Isbell and the 400 Unit. The music is emotionally evocative, pared down to just guitar and strings, with lyrics that embrace death because it makes each moment of a relationship both precious and desperate. This new take on a love song won Jason Isbell the 2018 Grammy for Best American Roots Song. Our brains value the familiarly new because it is comfortable, drawing on both auditory and emotional memories.

## OPENING PANDORA'S BOX

Our small-scale study predicting hit songs for Steereo motivated me to scale up our ability to understand and predict hit music. Music streaming services have invested in technologies to identify and introduce new music customized to subscribers' playlists. Spotify does this with Discover Weekly, a playlist of thirty new songs subscribers receive every Monday morning. Pandora classifies new music using 450 attributes in its Music Genome Project and introduces new music using a service called Personalized Soundtracks.

Tracking what people add to their playlists boosts the likelihood of songs showing up in related playlists, thereby building support needed to create a hit. Nevertheless, only 4% of new songs will become bona fide hits. Finding this 4% has been called the "Hit Song Science" problem. To date, humans' and artificial intelligence's ability to predict hits has been quite poor. One result of this is that people churn through different music streaming platforms hoping that one will consistently recommend music they love.

My group collaborated with the music streaming service Pandora to see if neural responses could predict hit songs. The research team at Pandora chose twenty-four songs on their service that varied from rock (Girl in Red's "Bad Idea"), to hip-hop (Roddy Rich's "The Box"), to EDM (Tones and I's "Dance Monkey"). The number of listens varied from four thousand (NLE Choppa's "Dekario") to more than thirty-two million ("Dance Monkey"). Pandora's staff identified the threshold for a hit as a song with more than 700,000 streams. My team recruited thirty-three people to listen to the songs in random order. Participants were mostly young, with an average age of twenty-four, and were balanced between men and women.

First, we analyzed the predictive ability of self-reported "liking" of songs. Participants reported that they "liked" familiar songs more than unfamiliar ones with a very high 0.87 correlation. This is the definition of a hit: the more people hear a song, the more they like it. Remember the song "Macarena"? It was a breakout hit in 1996. But by 2002, VH1 ranked "Macarena" as the number one "awesomely bad" one-hit wonder. (I bet the "Macarena" chorus is playing in your head right now.)

When music was unfamiliar, self-reported "liking" had zero ability to identify hits. But a song's average Immersion and peak Immersion predicted hits with 69% accuracy. This was not bad, but I thought we could do better. The traditional statistical model used to make this forecast poorly captures the inherent nonlinearities in neurologic data. Machine learning models do this much better. My team set up a horse race between half a dozen different machine learning approaches, and the best of these predicted which songs were hits with 97% accuracy by using only average Immersion and peak

Immersion for each song. As with the Steereo data, we also tested whether neurologic data for the first minute of a song could predict a hit. We found it could with 82% accuracy.

To ensure that the predictions were not just due to random chance, we also predicted other market measures of impact, including the number of plays of each song on Pandora and the number of days the song had been on Pandora's platform. These additional measures were also statistically associated with Immersion. Here's where it gets really interesting. Our analysis also showed that if producers remixed a moderately successful song with 200,000 listens to increase its Immersion 10%, it would gain more than one million additional streams. This would move it from "just okay" to a legitimate hit.

Pandora and other streaming services can substantially improve the integration of new music into subscribers' playlists by choosing music with high average Immersion. Measuring the brain responses to music can also guide music producers in order to increase the likelihood of hits. This is another application of Creative+. As neuroscience technologies become less expensive and more widespread, an app will be able to curate individuals' playlists to respond to their moods. Down in the dumps? A streaming service could send this person Pharrell Williams' song "Happy." Or, if the data show that people want to feel down for a bit, the service could send "When the Party's Over" by Billie Eilish. A machine learning algorithm might even stream different versions of these songs for different people. Streaming services still ask subscribers to decide what music they like or dislike. Neurotechnologies paired with machine learning can eliminate this friction by knowing what people will love and when to give it to them.

Some people think that science will inhibit the creative process. Nonsense. Science can only measure responses to entertainment if brilliant people create content. Producing entertainment, since its inception, has been a blend of art and science. Measuring Immersion during table reads, during editing, and while creating music simply adds objective measurement to the creation of art. As more creatives use neuroscience to improve entertainment, consumers benefit. They get better movies, better TV, and more enjoyable songs. Entertainment gets a bit more entertaining.

In the next chapter, we explore if education should become edutainment.

## TAKEAWAYS

1. Novelty in entertainment must be balanced with contextual familiarity.
2. The brain knows a hit TV show or song in the first minute, so creatives should ensure the beginning is excellent.
3. Engage superfans before and after entertainment release to leverage their social media impact in order to create hits.
4. Increase enjoyment and market impact of movies by adding screen time for the most emotionally compelling character, even if that person is not the protagonist.
5. Real-time neurotechnology paired with machine learning is poised to automatically recommend entertainment content to consumers based on their moods.

# CHAPTER 4

# EDUCATION AND TRAINING THAT STICKS

"Do you mind getting beat up a bit?"

The question made perfect sense when Lt. Lopez said that the "enemy combatants" were wearing black T-shirts. I had dressed in a black T-shirt, camo pants, and boots for a day of combat training with the US Army.

Sure, I'll play the role of enemy in a training exercise designed to prepare soldiers for the mountain redoubts of Afghanistan.

I did get body-slammed a couple of times, once having cactus spines driven into my thigh. This was painful but also weirdly fun for a nerd seeking a better understanding of effective training techniques.

After every simulated skirmish, the action paused for an immediate debrief using the "three right, three wrong" technique. Those involved in the action, as well as observers, identified three things that the soldiers did correctly and three things they needed to improve. Even the slightly injured scientist was encouraged to contribute.

The debrief is an essential part of the OODA loop, developed by military strategist Col. John Boyd. OODA stands for observe–orient–decide–act and is a cycle in which the "observe" and "orient" parts (the latter denoting analysis) may occur many times before one makes a decision and then acts on it. The after-action brief—what in the civilian world is called feedback—is essential to improving performance. Boyd's key insight was that performance improves when the OODA loop is shortened. Doing this requires having the right data.

Corporate training seldom has the clear metrics used in the military such as ECIA and EKIA (enemy captured in action, enemy killed in action). In the corporate world, we need to know how the return on training will increase productivity, increase retention, and increase sales. While these are all measurable, it may take a year to evaluate training effectiveness. Col. Boyd would be choking on his hamburger (he loved hamburgers) if a pilot had to wait a year to assess whether training was effective.

"Time is the dominant parameter. The pilot who goes through

the OODA cycle in the shortest time prevails because his opponent is caught responding to situations that have already changed." This was how the chief designer of the General Dynamics F-16 Fighting Falcon jet, Harry Hillaker, described the OODA cycle. Boyd was part of the design team for the F-16 and convinced Hillaker to apply the OODA approach to design, constantly experimenting, collecting data, and making incremental improvements. If this sounds familiar, OODA is the foundation for agile software development that has become the standard when creating new technologies. The key to both the OODA loop and agile is getting rapid feedback and responding to it.

Just like pilots and soldiers, teachers and trainers get better when they receive rapid and consistent feedback. Students, too, benefit from rapid feedback, whether preparing for spelling bees, doing algebra, or writing essays. Parents, school administrators, and training architects want to know whether the information being taught is "reaching" learners.

This chapter will take the basics of the OODA loop and apply it to education and training, but with a twist. My team started measuring Immersion in K–12 classrooms and corporate training centers to see if we could improve outcomes for learners. Our hope was that the right feedback would make learning more enjoyable and accelerate information acquisition.

## THE SIZE OF THE PROBLEM

Required training—hours of it. It is almost always awful. Too long, too boring, and not useful for most people's jobs. Estimates are that only 10% of employee training improves job performance. The average company in the US compels its employees to spend thirty-four hours in training annually at a cost of $1300 per person. Approximately one-half of this training is done in a traditional classroom with an instructor talking to (or at) employees. Almost none of this training has any impact: thirty-one hours out of the thirty-four are wasted. Every year. Training also has very little effect on job satisfaction or retention. Unless the three actually useful hours of training supercharge employees' productivity, one must conclude that corporate training is a waste of money. Sure, many surveys suggest otherwise, but one has to be suspicious of these "liking" data. After all, in many companies, training happens at a nice hotel with good food and plenty to drink. Who would have the chutzpah to say it's a waste?

How about education? The US Department of Education's own analysis shows the abysmal performance of public schools. Only about one-quarter of students are proficient in any of nine subjects that are measured in the congressionally mandated National Assessment of Educational Progress tests taken in the fourth, eighth, and twelfth grades. For example, only 11% of high school seniors have a reasonable understanding of US history. Advanced proficiency is rare for any subject, hovering around 3% nationally. Private schools do better, educating one-third to one-half of their students to proficiency, while students of color fare worse, often much worse.

How is it possible that in the twenty-first century, educators and trainers are so profoundly ineffective? There are some bright spots. South Korea is rated as having the best K–12 education, followed by Japan, Singapore, Finland, and the United Kingdom. The data show that students in these countries remember the material presented in class and understand it well enough to pass exams weeks later.

While test scores are not the only measure of learning, these countries are clearly getting something right. Creating effective education and training starts with getting learners to absorb and remember what they are being taught.

## WHY WE REMEMBER

The first time you met your romantic partner. The birth of your child. The destruction and death of September 11, 2001. They are seared into your memory.

Dr. Eric Kandel was awarded the 2000 Nobel Prize in Physiology or Medicine for identifying how the brain forms long-term memories. He showed that facts like your phone number, address, and your Social Security number are remembered for decades because their constant use strengthens connections between neurons.

Emotional memories supercharge this effect. Emotions are the currency of memory because they tag information as valuable. Emotionally tagged information is stored in the brain without the need for repetition. Think of new information as a soccer ball sitting inside your brain. The brain is wet so the soccer ball is slippery and hard to grab. Emotions are like spikes with grippy handles sticking out of the soccer ball. Even when wet, the handles make the ball easy to pick up. The longer the emotional spikes on the soccer ball, the easier it is to pull memories from your brain. Immersion puts emotional spikes into experiences.

In a study of seventy-five adults who were shown videos with new information, we sought to identify the factors that improve information recall. Videos were used in this experiment so that the delivery of information was identical for all participants. The traditional approach to assessing learning asks people if they "liked" the presentation. We included this question in our analysis and found a negative correlation (–0.25) between "liking" and information recall. In other words, the more people said they "liked" the presentation, the less they remembered. Immersion and recall? A powerful positive 0.60 correlation.

Immersive training attaches emotional spikes to information, increasing the ability to recall and use it.

Teachers and trainers can increase Immersion by drawing on the insights from the last two chapters. They can start a lesson with a human-scale story that has a crisis and genuine emotions. Then involve students in a dialogue, rather than bloviate in a monologue, so that students are part of the learning process. For example, I teach a first-year PhD course in mathematical statistics. Most lectures involve theorems and proofs, but I always start with a story of an obscure mathematician whose work helped develop the technique the class is learning. This narrative contextualizes the analysis by providing an example of a person solving a problem. I also use props, including oversized cards, plastic roulette wheels, and the occasional magic trick. My teaching evaluations for this "dry" topic are always excellent. In fact, every year—against my advice—some of my students take their new knowledge to Las Vegas to test their analytical skills. A few even win.

Neurologic responses capture two dimensions that can be modified to improve information recall: content and delivery. Content can be improved by measuring whether modifications increase or decrease Immersion. Instructors can vary the books, articles, and videos students are assigned to prepare for class and then determine the effectiveness of class discussions.

Delivery can also be measured and improved. Delivery can be isolated by having two or more people present the same content. The quality of delivery can be assessed by evaluating information recall one or two weeks after a class. The instructor for the class with the best recall should then be recorded to identify what she or he is doing that improves learner outcomes. For example, this instructor might be speaking more slowly or might call on learners more often. Improvement requires measurement as described in the OODA loop. Even if neural responses are not measured, classes can be recorded and analyzed for technique. The approaches used by teachers and trainers who consistently produce better outcomes should be codified and shared with others.

In addition to how content is organized and delivered, another factor is essential for effective outcomes: readiness to learn.

## READINESS TO LEARN

Teachers get too much and too little credit for student outcomes. Part of the problem is that teachers receive too little feedback too slowly, and it is often of the wrong type. Asking students to evaluate a professor, as most colleges do, makes little sense unless the grade the student received (or expects to receive) is taken into account. Students will almost always say a teacher is "great" if they are getting a good grade and will say he or she is "god-awful" if they are doing poorly.

Some teachers are naturally interesting and interested in teaching; others, not so much. Some students are ready to learn; others struggle to sit still for an hour. Surveys of students, soldiers, and athletes relate learning readiness to attention, emotional regulation, and resiliency. But...surveys.

I wanted an objective measure of whether someone was ready to listen, learn, and participate. Such a technology could give teachers and trainers real-time feedback that could help learners improve their outcomes instead of failing a test.

I developed and calibrated a readiness-to-learn measure that I call physiologic psychological safety. The idea of psychological safety has been around for quite a while and is traditionally measured using surveys; an especially well-known one was developed by Amy Edmonson at Harvard Business School. You can think of physiologic psychological safety as the opposite of anxiety. One of my management-thinker heroes is W. Edwards Deming who wrote in 1982, "Drive out fear, so that everyone may work effectively for the company." This also applies to training. When learners are psychologically safe, they acquire new information easily because they have the cognitive and emotional bandwidth to concentrate on course material. Anxiety takes significant metabolic energy and inhibits learning. The innovation in my measure of psychological safety is that it is passive, continuous, and objective. No survey needed.

Education innovator and my friend Flip Flippen has said

that teachers need to "capture kids' hearts" before they can engage their minds. His company trains teachers to assess and increase psychological safety to improve learning outcomes. A daily assessment happens when teachers greet each student by name and with a handshake. This personal connection signals to students that they are valued and safe. In a randomized controlled trial, the students of teachers trained in these techniques had a 40% increase in social skills, including respect, caring for others, and problem-solving; and they had a 22% decrease in disciplinary referrals compared to control schools.

A variety of factors hinder psychological safety. Hunger and a lack of sleep are on top of the list. So are negative social interactions, physical and psychological trauma, and illicit drug use. Genetics plays a role in anxiety as does depression or depressive symptoms. For adults, facing financial straits, job loss, medical disorders, divorce, and death of a loved one all increase anxiety. Even too much caffeine can inhibit one's readiness to learn by putting someone on edge physiologically.

Once I had identified the physiologic range in which people are psychologically safe and unsafe, I needed to see how effective it was in predicting student outcomes to ensure it was useful. One of my former graduate students landed his first job teaching economics at an elite college in the northeastern United States. He agreed to measure neurologic responses in his class of twenty-three students for eight classes prior to the midterm. Averaging physiologic psychological safety for each student across classes revealed a strong positive association with grades. A 25% increase in psychological safety increased students' midterm performance by a full letter grade.

The analysis also showed no relationship between average Immersion and grades. Let's be honest; Economics 101 can only be made moderately interesting by even the best professors. Data from multiple studies analyzed by my team have shown that psychological safety is the precursor to Immersion. If people are not relaxed, they do not have the metabolic energy to be immersed in an experience. Moreover, it is critical that diverse individuals feel comfortable in the physical space and social context of a learning experience. Creating a safe environment is also important when people are stressed by being required to take a course and will be evaluated on the material in it.

If psychological safety is low, interventions such as a short meditation, a break, or exercise can often reset the brain and burn off energy in order to open enough bandwidth to learn. Noise induces stress, and simply soundproofing classrooms has a salubrious effect on grades. Getting enough sleep is vital as well. In 2019, California became the first state to push back the start of high school to 8:30 a.m. School districts that have moved high school start times an hour later have seen a substantial improvement in students' attendance and grades.

## IMMERSIVE TEACHING

When my team assessed the effect of neurologic frustration on students' Economics 101 midterm performance, we found that average frustration for the eight classes before the midterm had a statistically negative impact on grades. Examining the minute-by-minute data showed long periods of frustration. It was clear that the class was causing students to tune out. So, how can instructors avoid neurologic frustration?

There are a number of ways frustration can be reduced or eliminated. The best way is to design consistent student participation into the curriculum. This can be done using polls and group projects, and by running in-class experiments. Prompting the lazy brain to remain immersed requires activity and novelty. Learning is facilitated by changing what students do to gain competency and through social interactions among learners. Instructors teaching in person do this naturally by scanning the room to see if students appear to be engaged. It is more difficult to assess student engagement during online teaching. This is where technology that measures responses in real time can radically improve student outcomes by showing instructors when they need to adjust classwork to fit the needs of students.

"Flipped" classrooms are a type of blended learning in which students read material and watch lectures before class. Class time is then focused on solving problems, with the teacher coaching students as they try to apply what they are learning. This shortens the OODA loop and thereby accelerates learning. Meteor Education in Florida creates specially designed classrooms that enable teachers to more effectively coach students doing active learning tasks. When teachers change what students do every fifteen to twenty minutes, the data show that middle school and high school students can sustain Immersion for an hour.

Part of the OODA process asks students to reflect on what they learned. In the best case, the students who learned the most are called upon to lead these discussions. If you want to learn to swim, better to ask the Olympian rather than the kid taking his first lessons at the YMCA. Instructors can identify students who have mastered the material in flipped classrooms by the statements they make. This can also be done using technology that identifies the most immersed students, often with surprising results.

Meteor Education introduced the Immersion platform to a middle school in a low-income neighborhood in Southern California. Mrs. Rodriguez, a fifth-grade teacher, invited me to observe her class. She told me how ranking students by Immersion in real time had identified a girl named Maria as a math superfan. Maria did not ask any questions in math class, and Mrs. Rodriguez originally thought she was uninterested. Mrs. Rodriguez told me that when the data showed that Maria was the most immersed student three days in a row, she approached her after class. Maria lit up and said that math was her favorite subject. With Mrs. Rodriguez's encouragement, Maria was often the discussion leader in math because she could effectively explain concepts to the other children. Being called on regularly, Mrs. Rodriguez told me, helped Maria come out of her shell and interact socially. It also helped the other children to have a peer explain what was being done. The OODA cycle is shortened when discussion leaders understand material well enough to explain it to others.

Leaderboards are used in many settings, especially in video games, to motivate performance. They can also form the basis for gamification. Those on top of the leaderboard can get physical or virtual badges that say, "Ask Me About Algebra" or "Talk To Me About Chemistry." The same approach can be used during employee training. Imagine how interesting a corporate training event would be if, during a break, you saw a person with a badge saying, "Ask Me How To Double Sales" or "Ask Me About Accounting Innovations." The badge stimulates conversation about the topic, reinforcing the training so all learners "level up."

Those who are struggling to get badges should not be blamed or shamed. There are many reasons why material may not land well in someone's brain. As we discussed, low psychological safety tops the list. Neurologic frustration could also be due to a disinterested, ill-prepared, or boring presenter. Finally, the material may be abstruse or poorly structured, making it difficult to understand. Identifying those on the bottom of the leaderboard using technology provides an opportunity to help learners become proficient before waiting for them to fail a test. Struggling students could be given a link to a Khan Academy lesson or they could be offered a tutor. Adult learners who are not immersed in training could be emailed additional material or offered a seat at a refresher course or webinar.

## INSIGHTS FROM IMMERSIVE TRAINING

It is tough to sit in a classroom all day in the go-go world in which we live. Forward-thinking companies are hitting back, creating new ways to present information that seek to bolster learning. My team ran several studies to see if innovative training approaches are really better.

Our first investigation was a partnership with a Los Angeles–based startup called Caseworx. Caseworx produces videos in which actors dramatize contextual narratives to illustrate vital business information. The videos show, rather than tell, what people need to learn. Caseworx's first videos depicted information in Harvard Business School case studies, the definitive source material for university business courses.

We measured Immersion while one half of a class of college students read a Harvard Business School case. The other half watched a Caseworx video that depicted the same information portrayed as a story. The data showed that the video was 14% more immersive than the written case, reduced neurologic frustration by 75%, and produced 11% more peak Immersion. Importantly, higher Immersion produced better outcomes for students. Students who watched the Caseworx video were able to recall 97% more information compared to those who read the case. Students also reported that watching the video was 59% more enjoyable than reading. This shows how profoundly the presentation of material, not just the content itself, improves outcomes. These findings also reinforce the primacy of narrative for information transmission as we discussed in Chapter 2.

The data also confirm the Ferris Bueller effect: neurologic frustration obstructed knowledge retention (correlation $-0.78$) and reduced enjoyment (correlation $-0.37$). These insights validate Caseworx's story-based videos as an effective way to convey information. While students can watch Caseworx videos by themselves, they are typically presented in a classroom and are followed by a facilitated discussion that reinforces key points and improves recall even more. Justin Wolske, CEO of Caseworx, said, "Measuring efficacy in learning is notoriously difficult, and neuroscience gave us a way to frame the discussion that was relatable to educators. It was also great to see for ourselves that what we're doing was making an impact."

We also had a chance to evaluate simulations as a learning approach by collaborating with Ed Leadership SIMS (ELS). ELS's platform uses branching simulations to help teachers and school administrators prepare for circumstances that may arise during their duties. The simulations allow learners to replay the scenarios and see how different decisions lead to different outcomes.

ELS measured Immersion while administrators attended training in Iowa. Participants were split into two groups. The first group explored scenarios using ELS simulations while the second group read and discussed a written case. The data showed that attendees were 10% more immersed in simulations compared to reading cases. Simulations also generated 12% more peak experiences. These data show that active tasks are an effective way to convey information to learners.

These findings were confirmed in a study I did with Jeff Dieffenbach and his colleagues at the MIT Integrated Learning Initiative. We collected neurologic data at the Masie Learning Conference, a well-respected annual event for training professionals. We compared Immersion and productivity as individuals or teams earned points in a trivia-recall task. Immersion averaged across teams of four was positively related to points earned (correlation 0.29), while individual performance was unrelated to Immersion. Singletons had no one with whom to engage in give-and-take, diminishing their productivity. As social creatures, we nearly always perform better when others are around us. Even elite athletes achieve peak performance when they represent their country at the Olympics. If these results reflected higher team productivity at work, a midsize company with annual revenues of $100 million would earn an additional $9 million every year by creating high-Immersion work teams.

These findings suggest being cautious of the "learn whenever you want" approach. If individuals have a rough sense of when they feel sufficiently psychologically safe to learn, learning using asynchronous modules can be effective. But the social aspect of learning increases Immersion and thus improves information retention, raising the return on training. Sharing information with a group and motivating others to perform at peak levels is precisely what social creatures do. Learning in teams is most effective when the trainer establishes psychological safety, when groups are not too large (generally ten people or fewer), and when learning is active.

But even active learning needs structure.

## THE 20-20-20 RULE

The multinational professional services company Accenture produces over fifteen million hours of training for their employees at a cost of $1 billion annually. They have talented teams of learning architects and designers who deliver twenty-four thousand courses to "future-proof" employees' careers. Their training starts with onboarding new associates and goes all the way to teaching leadership techniques to directors. An investment of $1 billion is significant for a company with $43 billion in annual revenue.

Accenture's internally facing Talent Research and Innovation team experimented with the structure of meetings and the presentation of information in order to raise the return on training. Learning designers would wait six to twelve months to see if newly trained employees' billable hours increased. Their learning team used a "guess and verify" method: Should training be held for one day or two? Should sessions last forty-one minutes, or sixty, or ninety-two? Working lunch or lunch break? They experimented with innumerable changes and then waited to see what happened. There were so many variables in play that it was nearly impossible to relate changes in course design to post-training performance metrics. What the company needed was a real-time measure of training effectiveness that predicted outcomes from training. These needs led to my partnership with Accenture, which resulted in thousands of hours of neurologic data that we have mined for insights.

The data showed that hour-long sessions without participation are Immersion killers. No matter how exciting, engaging, funny, moving, or talented a speaker is, the longer she or he is on stage, the more the audience's Immersion erodes. Accenture found that the deterioration in Immersion could be reversed by creating opportunities for learner participation. When a speaker asks the audience to reflect on delivered content, Immersion increases. When a speaker asks learners to discuss new material with their peers, Immersion increases even more. And Immersion increases the most when a speaker asks learners to solve a problem or create something with new information.

Accenture also found that lunch sessions, even those that feature dialogues with senior leaders, produce neural fatigue. Without time to rest, the first session after a working lunch also has low Immersion. People need a cognitive and emotional recovery period before their brains are able to re-engage and learn. Meals provide a chance for learners to rebuild energy stores and so does time to socialize. Accenture now schedules in more breaks between sessions so learners are able to fully immerse themselves during training. Recovery can occur in as little as ten minutes, so breaks can be short but should be frequent.

Accenture's team also discovered that something that nearly every meeting does is a waste of time: introductions. The data show that everyone except for the person speaking is neurologically frustrated during these recitations. Instead of an introduction, Accenture now puts names on paper tents in front of attendees. Using name tents also avoids "introduction creep" in which one person offers an in-depth description of his or her job, career and personal goals, sporting activities, children, and dog. People are able to meet each other during frequent breaks without formal introductions.

Accenture's data has led them to create what I call the 20-20-20 rule. There is a twenty-minute presentation of information followed by twenty minutes for attendees to apply the information and twenty minutes to debrief on what people learned. Add another twenty for a break to increase psychological safety and the cycle restarts.

Accenture's team has captured video of their training sessions, both in-person and online. Immersion data are overlaid on the video to determine how to optimize content and delivery. This approach allows them to structure training so that the most important information occurs during Immersion peaks to ensure it enters into memory. Peak Immersion moments are created by presenting information using a narrative arc, changing media types regularly, and including participatory tasks.

Accenture also uses real-time neural responses to radically shorten the OODA loop for sales training. During a sales training session, a participant practices a sales pitch in front of his or her colleagues while Immersion is displayed in real time providing immediate feedback from trainers. The data show when Immersion trends upward, indicating an effective pitch, and when Immersion drops, indicating that it is time for a pivot. These data are immediately viewable and objective. Among learning professionals this is known as RTF (real-time feedback) or FML (feedback microlearning) and is the most effective way to improve rapidly. Accenture's senior talent innovation lead, Bob Gerard, told me that having neural data to back up changes in learning approaches made it easier to persuade stakeholders that training had improved and that changes were creating value for the company.

Learning architects have three measurable dimensions that can improve outcomes: content, delivery, and readiness. Better measurement produces better outcomes. And faster measurement improves outcomes faster.

## GOING VIRAL

If any group has elevated the art of presentation, it is the curators of the TED conferences. The eighteen-minute TED presentation has been adopted by corporations, schools, and governments. To reinforce best practices, TED sends its speakers the "TED Commandments." These include: Thou

Shalt Reveal Thy Curiosity and Thy Passion; Thou Shalt Be Vulnerable; and Thou Shalt Tell a Story. These commandments are valuable advice for any speaker.

I spoke at TED Global in 2011 and had eight months to prepare, workshop, and improve my talk before I hit the stage in Edinburgh, Scotland. My own metrics for a successful talk at TED were getting a standing ovation when speaking live and having millions of people view the talk online. I achieved both of these milestones as have many others.

After watching hundreds of TED Talks, I have identified a number of core principles to giving an extraordinary presentation. Let's be clear: speaking in public is hard. During my rehearsal at TED Global, I was so nervous that I could not speak and advance my slides at the same time. If you look at my talk carefully, you will notice that I am not holding a remote in my hand; the stage manager had to use my script to change the slides for me.

As my team began to collect Immersion data at live events, I discovered that many of the TED Commandments drive up Immersion. The first thing we found, just as Accenture had, was that shorter talks are nearly always better. An hour is a long time for anyone to pay attention and be emotionally engaged in a presentation. The TED conference recently introduced five-minute talks. A super-short talk can be quite good, but it must be structured to keep audiences immersed.

Whether speaking for five, eighteen, or sixty minutes, speakers need a hot open, often using a provocative statement. Comedian Jerry Seinfeld has said the same thing about comedy:

the worst thing a comedian can do is to open with "How are you doing tonight?" This diffuses the pent-up anticipation of the audience while waiting for the comedian's performance. Speakers should use the power of anticipation by starting with a statement that directs the audience's energy into the talk, not by saying something lame. I add energy to the room by running onto the stage. This also helps me calm down by burning off some of my excitement.

Talks need to be memorized, rehearsed, and structured around a clear narrative arc with a beginning, middle, and end. Many speakers dissipate the audience's energy by "burying the lead" of their talk. This happens when talks are structured chronologically using a "first I did this, then I did that" approach. Put the lead out front by saying, "I discovered this thing" or "I was able to do this thing." Put emotion behind it, put energy into it, and Immersion will spike. That's when you can go backward and tell the story of how you reached your discovery or accomplished your goal.

The audience's energy can be concentrated by using a speaker's most difficult gambit: silence. Our studies show that pauses of two seconds or longer nearly always cause Immersion peaks as soon as the talk resumes. Silence also allows the audience to more effectively process presented information, increasing retention and comprehension. An easy way to create a strategic pause is to pose a question and then wait while audience members think about an answer. To get the pause right, after asking a question, do a slow count to three in your head before speaking again. Very confident speakers will take the stage and wait for a couple of beats to build anticipation before starting to speak. Movie directors also know the power of silence. Martin Scorsese is a master of quiet; watch *Raging Bull* or *Goodfellas* and note how silence builds anticipation for a scene to resolve.

Immersion data at live events has also established that mixing media impels Immersion upward, especially for long talks. When a speaker shows pictures or videos, it interrupts the neurologic monotony of speaking. Our studies show that videos are particularly immersive. But you shouldn't take this too far. In my experience, four to five short videos during an hour-long presentation are as much as one should use. I learned from TED that any media you use, whether static or dynamic, should have few or no words to explain them; the speaker should be the one to explain what is shown.

Here's a hack: several studies from my lab have shown that coordinated movement (dancing, singing, marching) increases Immersion. We have measured Immersion in churches, at folk dances, while soldiers march, and even with Indigenous people dancing in Papua New Guinea. The movement-Immersion link occurs everywhere. Think about what athletes do before a match—they warm up. You can get attendees at a conference to warm up cognitively and emotionally through movement. Sitting for an hour in a small chair is uncomfortable, so create a reason for people to get up and move. This could be as simple as clapping in rhythm. A speaker I saw at the GroupM Huddle in Copenhagen opened her talk by asking people to hug each other. I was collecting data and sure enough, Immersion spiked even as the room erupted in nervous laughter.

If the room is not too large, you can build Immersion with

audience participation. I sometimes go into the audience to interact with people during Q and A sessions or toss squishy foam brains to audience members who bravely ask questions. For longer presentations, assign audience members to do something in small groups. Some of these people will be Immersion superfans and will often volunteer to report their table's findings. You can put them in the spotlight and have them share what they have learned.

Let's move our sights up from good to great: how can you make a talk go viral? To find out, my team picked TED Talks that, according to online lists, are the best and worst. The most-watched TED talk we measured was by Brené Brown and has more than thirty-eight million views, while the talk with the fewest views, under 5,000, was by a nonprofit executive. And no, I did not include my own talk because we ran the study in Claremont, California, and many participants there have seen it.

Consistent with the data we'd collected at live events, higher Immersion during TED Talks predicted more online views (correlation 0.37). A 10% increase in Immersion would result in 16% more online views of a talk. The median number of views for more than twenty-five hundred TED talks is 1.1 million. This means that a speaker who is able to increase Immersion by 10% will get 176,000 more online views—a massive effect.

We also found a negative association between neurologic frustration and views (correlation –0.21). Frustration probably does more than just stop people from enjoying TED Talks; frustration likely causes viewers to stop watching, just as we discussed regarding entertainment in Chapter 3. The TED Foundation does not report how long one must watch a talk for it to count as a "view," but YouTube uses "around thirty seconds." If TED included a minimum watching time for a "view," the reported views for many talks would be lower since people will quit watching if they are neurologically frustrated.

In order to understand what makes some TED talks extraordinary, we examined the longest and highest moments of peak Immersion. The data showed eighteen peak Immersion periods of twenty-four seconds or longer. Remember that peak Immersion is metabolically expensive for the brain, so a twenty-four-second peak is unusual. These long peaks varied from one for Brené Brown to five for Tony Robbins. The peaks showed that speakers were able to create powerful moments when they shared personal stories, when they did something completely unexpected (sometimes by varying media, for example, showing a short film or doing a demonstration), and during calls to action when audiences were told things they could do to improve their lives.

## VIRTUAL MEETINGS

This chapter is being written during the COVID-19 pandemic. Quite quickly, meeting planners learned that running a remote event is not like running an in-person meeting. Virtual meetings need to be structured to keep people immersed when the social pressure of being in a room together is missing. I combed through post-COVID Immersion data to identify best practices when running remote events. Here's what that data show:

- Have all attendees turn on their cameras.
- Summarize ground rules for the meeting, including when discussions will occur and how group work will be done.
- Call attendees by name.
- Lead a short meditation or breathing exercise to establish psychological safety.
- Presenters should speak for no more than fifteen minutes before getting feedback from attendees.
- Vary media types.
- Show fewer static slides and instead write key points dynamically on a virtual white board.
- Create virtual breakout rooms where attendees can apply new knowledge in small groups.
- Identify those who have mastered new information and can best facilitate peer discussion.
- Gamify meetings using virtual badges for the most immersed attendees.
- Use more frequent, shorter meetings—for example, thirty minutes twice a day—rather than one hour a day.
- Get feedback from larger groups using polls.
- Leverage the consolidation of information during sleep by giving attendees a task to do overnight.

Distributed work is not going away. Blended meetings are the norm from now on. It's a new remote-work world, so it is essential to ensure that virtual meetings are effective. Remember that content, delivery, and readiness together affect Immersion and the efficacy of training, education, and meetings.

## KEY TAKEAWAYS

1. Three dimensions determine how effectively information is transmitted: content, delivery, and readiness.
2. Establish psychological safety to ensure readiness to learn; mindfulness meditation or a break is an effective reset.
3. Use the 20-20-20 rule to sustain Immersion and increase information recall.
4. The most important information should be presented during Immersion peaks.
5. Learners in teams outperform learners alone.

# CHAPTER 5

# ATTRACTIONS AND RETAIL THAT AMAZE

Pirates of the Caribbean. I have no doubt it's the best.

Southern Californians have an ongoing debate: which ride at Disneyland is best? Most of us who live near Disneyland have been going there since we were kids and as adults enjoy the Happiest Place on Earth with our kids. Disney offers a Southern California annual pass that is discounted for people who can go at lower-traffic times like midweek and winter, so most locals have lots of Disneyland experience. Could we use science to figure out which attraction is really the best?

One of the foundational innovations made by Walt Disney and his Imagineers was to wrap each attraction around a story. Disney Imagineers call this type of entertainment a narrative experience. Space Mountain, a roller coaster you ride in the dark, is wrapped around a narrative of space travel in which guests enter a space station, are instructed on their mission, and see special effects as they whiz around the track. Importantly, it is not just the rides themselves that are a narrative experience; the queue to enter the attraction has story elements that make the wait less onerous and build anticipation for the adventure.

My team and I went to Disneyland and used an app on our mobile phones to capture Immersion. We went midweek and could not test every ride because some were closed for maintenance. There were only four of us, two men and two women, so this was a semi-scientific study.

Every ride we went on generated Immersion above the 98th percentile compared to several thousand live experiences that we had measured. The Disney Imagineers know their stuff. Counter to my expectation, Space Mountain—not Pirates of the Caribbean—was the most immersive attraction. The second-highest-Immersion ride was Splash Mountain, a log flume ride at the time based on characters and songs from the 1946 Disney film *Song of the South* (featuring the song "Zip-a-Dee-Doo-Dah"). It ends with a fifty-foot drop that drenches riders with water. I was in the front seat and was soaked down to my underwear—it was a blast.

Where was Pirates of the Caribbean? For our group it was dead last, producing Immersion that was 19% lower than Space Mountain; Pirates even had 10% lower Immersion than Mr. Toad's Wild Ride, an attraction for the six and under set. Pirates' Immersion was hurt by its having only a few peak immersion moments. This demonstrates again that intuition blows when data flows.

The data also showed that queuing up for rides created Immersion in the 90th percentile. This confirms Walt Disney's narrative-driven design. Indeed, averaging all the attractions we went on, Immersion while entering nearly equaled Immersion during the rides. Waiting to get on an older roller coaster, Thunder Mountain Railroad, was more immersive than the ride itself!

In the twenty-first century when many of us can enjoy unlimited entertainment online, why are people leaving the house all?

The answer is that the experience economy is most valuable when one has an actual experience. This chapter examines why 80% of retail sales still occur in brick-and-mortar stores and shows how to create extraordinary experiences for customers. This chapter will explain how to create consumer experiences that are as good as Disneyland's, peaking Immersion so that people willingly spend their time and money for something extraordinary.

## NARRATIVE CUSTOMER JOURNEY

Environmental psychology scrutinizes how people interact in designed environments. In the 1970s, environmental psychologists, most prominently Paco Underhill, measured how retail store design affected the way people shopped and how much they purchased. These studies are the reason why every supermarket puts milk in the back of the store. People purchase milk regularly, and this design forces them to walk the length of the store during every trip. Along the way, they are likely to see more items that they need or want. The term of art for this type of design is *building the basket*.

A major US telecommunications provider embraced environmental psychology by having "shopping anthropologists" observe customers in their retail stores. They identified "sticky" areas where people spent the most time and laid these out linearly to slow down customers as they walked through their stores. This was a simple application of the "milk in the back of the market" design. The company's leadership was so convinced that customers would be absorbed by the new layout that they reduced sales associates by one-third.

The backlash was immediate: customers were angry because they had to wait for help to buy a new phone or to change a service plan. The company asked us to figure out what had gone wrong.

We invited customers to participate in a study collecting neurologic and visual data as they shopped in the company's stores in San Francisco, California, and Austin, Texas. Visual fixations were collected using eye-tracking glasses that had two cameras, one facing the wearer's eyes and the other facing outward. This allowed for precise identification of what each person was looking at and for how long. The eye-tracking glasses we used cost $30,000. Here's a tip: you can get nearly the same data quality by buying a $200 GoPro camera and a $10 head strap. Eye-tracking data alone, like the observations of shopping anthropologists, cannot distinguish whether someone is looking at a display or merchandise because it is neurologically interesting or because a person is frustrated. Without neurologic data, one cannot differentiate a "good" visual fixation from a "bad" one.

The highest-Immersion parts of the store experience occurred when people looked at the newest goodies, especially cell phones and headphones. People were nearly always visually fixating on high-Immersion items, but we still discovered several fixations that were neurologically frustrating. The highest-frustration parts of the experience were looking for phone cases and evaluating bundled internet and phone plans.

Environmental psychologists simply timed how long people stopped in each area and were thus unable to differentiate between Immersion and frustration. This resulted in a poor store design and unhappy customers. Our study caused the company to reorganize their stores once again. We developed a map that laid out displays for key purchase types that built Immersion as customers journeyed through stores, creating a narrative experience. Immersion in a display slows down customers and is also a key step toward a purchase.

Customers can navigate the store on their own when there is a visual hierarchy that guides them through the narrative. The customer journey can have branches that lead to phones or broadband bundles or routers, with each path illustrating how the product has improved the lives of users. The narrative needs to be at human scale, show the emotional toll when telecom service is subpar, and lead the customer to a solution that resolves the crisis and produces happiness. Even nonprofits need to create narrative journeys to entice patrons. The Peabody Essex Museum in Massachusetts hired a full-time neuroscientist in 2017 to craft immersive journeys for visitors.

The end point of a narrative-driven customer journey should be high-Immersion displays for items that also have high profit margins. This is the point at which a sales associate should approach customers and close a sale. Our analysis showed that such a store design would keep the average customer shopping for a few extra minutes with less frustration. This produces a more enjoyable customer experience and lifts sales.

This narrative experience approach transforms retail from volume-focused to an experience of discovery. Apple's Town Square stores do this by having comfortable places to sit, huge screens, and tree-lined Genius Groves. Nordstrom's compact Local stores do not carry any merchandise to purchase. Instead, stylists personalize the experience and guide shoppers to buy online. Narrative retail venues have become destinations for shoppers and nonshoppers alike. Topping this list is Bass Pro Shops. I have gone there many times for lunch and to enjoy the experience, and nearly always end up buying products along the way. So far, I've resisted buying a boat, but eventually I just might enjoy the shopping so much that I make a big purchase. Bass Pro Shops uses narratives to build emotional connections with shoppers who go there simply for the pleasure.

## SELF-SERVICE SHOPPING

Once one has chosen where to shop, how can companies make the customer experience extraordinary? The first step is to identify the immersive parts of a typical shopping trip. We recruited people to shop at a major retailer and asked them to record their journey on their cell phone cameras. As we discussed in Chapter 3, long data collections cause Immersion to stay near its average. As a result, our analysis focused on what caused Immersion to peak and plummet.

We found that liquor was the most immersive part of shopping.

Perhaps this is not surprising since many shoppers associate alcohol with enjoyable experiences. Immersion has a halo effect, so putting alcohol in the front of the store could improve shoppers' moods, causing them to spend more freely. Shopping for nonalcoholic beverages also peaked Immersion, though less than for alcohol. Our sample was biased toward younger shoppers who tend to drink more than older people, but this result was found in all age groups.

The beauty aisle produced a split decision: it generated both peak Immersion moments and high frustration, particularly in women who spent the most time in this area. As the father of two girls, I can attest that shopping for personal care products causes rapid fluctuations between joy and misery. The excessive number of items in the beauty aisle leads to what psychologist Barry Schwartz has called the "paradox of choice" in which too many options cause anxiety. Our data support this.

Frustration emerged when people could not find the correct aisle and when products they wanted were not available. That is no surprise. One of the most frustrating moments was waiting in the check-out line. Displaying better signage, having more cashiers or self-checkouts, and restocking shelves would reduce frustration and improve the shopping experience.

What we had left out was the role of human interactions during shopping. Our next study examined that.

## LUXURY SHOPPING

The importance of customer service is acutely felt in retail sales.

Brick-and-mortar retail is struggling. In the US, the number of department store locations peaked in 2011 at 8,625 and had dropped to less than 6,000 by 2021, and the downward trend is expected to continue. The COVID-19 lockdowns in 2020 to 2021 accelerated the retail apocalypse as entire malls closed and major retailers, including JCPenney, Neiman Marcus, Stein Mart, and Lord & Taylor, were pushed into bankruptcy. Yet Market Track reports that a majority of people prefer to shop in stores rather than online because of the service they receive. Retail stores need to create fabulous customer experiences in order to differentiate themselves from both their physical and online competitors and to create loyal customers.

Be honest: at least once in a while, an amazing sales associate gets you to buy more than you had planned. You are not alone: 54% of customers purchased more products or services because of a great experience. On the other hand, you may have sworn off a store because of bad service—58% of people who have had a bad experience stop shopping at the store where they were maltreated. One of the most effective ways for sales associates to build emotional connections with repeat customers is to greet them by name.

My team wanted to figure out what makes a great customer experience and how this drives sales. Zappos, famous for their extraordinary phone service, calls this making a PEC or Personal Emotional Connection. Could we capture PECs while people shopped? And could neurologic Immersion predict whether people purchased or not? We carried out a study at two luxury clothing stores to find out.

Because Immersion captures social value, it is contagious.

If you are immersed in me and what I'm doing, I'll become immersed in you and what you are doing. We hypothesized that this would be true for sales associates and their customers. If sales associates love helping people, then their customers might absorb their Immersion and vice versa. Immersion contagion gives us a way to measure neurologic responses without bothering customers by asking them to wear a sensor. Our study had sales associates wear an Apple Watch with the Immersion app installed while they served customers. Since each shopping experience is unique, we really had no idea if neurologic data would predict purchases.

We collected Immersion data while customers shopped at either a high-end men's clothing store or a nearby store that sold fashionable women's clothes. Both were owned by the same company that gave us permission to collect data. We also videotaped customer interactions and overlaid the Immersion data on the videos to understand the parts of the customer journey that generated peak Immersion.

The average client spent twenty-three minutes and twenty-three seconds in the stores. The longest encounter was two hours and eleven minutes during which a female customer purchased $2,711 worth of women's clothing. Sixty-four percent of customers made purchases and the average spend was $328. Across both stores, average Immersion was 16% higher than the live experience benchmark. Peak Immersion was also high, nearly double the benchmark. Our first takeaway was that customers were having fantastic shopping experiences.

We estimated a statistical model to predict which customers would make a purchase. The model identified who would buy with 69% accuracy using sales associates' average Immersion when serving each customer. When we added the time customers spent in the store, the model's predictive accuracy increased to 84%. All this without bothering customers to ask how "satisfied" they were.

Here's the most important finding: the amount customers spent increased linearly with the sales associate's Immersion. We confirmed Zappos' sales approach: when the experience between customer and sales associate generates a PEC, sales rise. The model showed that for an average customer, a 50% increase in Immersion would result in an additional $43 of purchases. This is the power of authentic emotional connection.

In order to identify what happens during extraordinary customer experiences, we clipped out the epochs in the videos when Immersion peaked. Peaks appeared when sales associates shared product narratives, gave recommendations for purchases and personal advice, and surprised customers by offering a refreshment or carrying their shopping bags. Each one of these parts of the selling ceremony can be made immersive with measurement and practice in order to connect to customers on an emotional level. The retail apocalypse may still be happening, but individual stores can buck this trend by training sales associates to provide immersive customer experiences that will not only close sales, but generate a desire to return to shop again.

## SHOPPING AND BILLBOARDS

So far, we've looked at the in-store shopping experience, but what about the customer's journey before they even get to a store? Companies worldwide spent $32 billion on outdoor advertising in 2021, spending that has been increasing by $1 billion each year. An average company will spend about 10% of their marketing budget on outdoor promotion. Billboards, both poster and digital, are in your face. But are they effective?

The global outdoor advertising company JCDecaux asked my team to help them measure how effectively their billboards were getting into shoppers' brains. We thought the study should be done in a busy urban space with substantial competing stimulation. So we jetted off to Copenhagen and set up in one of its busiest shopping districts, Nørreport.

The impact of outdoor advertising is generally assessed by the number of "impressions" it produces. Impressions depend on how many people walk and drive by and are estimated to see the billboard. We wanted to measure the impact of outdoor advertising by directly measuring how many people actually saw the billboard, how long they saw it, and how immersive the information was to their brains. As in the study of the telecom retailer, we paired wearable sensors to measure Immersion with eye-tracking glasses. Participants were asked to walk a specific route in Nørreport and were instructed to notice any advertising on their journey. The walk took about three minutes.

The analysis showed that outdoor advertising averaged around two and a half seconds of visual fixation for an average of two looks per billboard. This brief visual burst was enough to generate an Immersion spike. All the JCDecaux billboards in Nørreport are digital and generated an average neurologic

Immersion that was 21% above the advertising benchmark. This confirms the value of outdoor advertising, since Immersion and information recall are positively correlated.

The data showed that moderate foot traffic produced the highest Immersion in billboards. This is contrary to the supposition that "impressions" increase linearly with traffic. Our study found that Immersion was low with light foot traffic as people walked quickly and did not scan the periphery where billboards are located. On the other end of the spectrum, areas and times with heavy pedestrian traffic occluded billboards while visual attention was focused on avoiding other people rather than on advertising. This "Goldilocks effect" meant that the highest Immersion occurred when there were enough people around that one had to scan the environment, but not so many that the information was crowded out by masses of humanity.

Retailers can use these findings to attract customers to their stores. This study also suggests that store signage is most effective when there are a moderate number of customers walking by. When foot traffic is very light or very heavy, people are either going directly to their destination or are watching others to avoid bumping into them. At these times, stores should put a smiling sales associate in front of the store to greet people. As social creatures, we fixate on other humans. This pulls visual attention to the store and can entice people to enter and shop. This is less important when foot traffic is moderate because people are able to see signage as they scan the environment.

## CUSTOMER LOYALTY

Loyalty is profitable. A study by Experian reported that three out of four US customer loyalty programs produce a positive return on investment. Yet the same study found that 64% of companies need better data to improve the customer experience. This disconnect is often due to how loyalty programs are implemented.

In 2015 American Express launched a rewards program aggregator called Plenti. Plenti members earned points for purchases at retailers such as ExxonMobil, Rite Aid, Walmart, and Macy's whether they used an American Express card or not. Accumulated points were translated into dollars that could be used at member stores. Retailers signed on because they saved the expense of running their own loyalty programs, and customers benefited by having more choices.

Plenti was based on a fabulous idea: points earned for necessities like gas and groceries could be used to reward oneself with a new sweater or pair of pants. A rollout in Europe showed that receiving unexpected rewards was the key to the Plenti experience. Cashiers at member companies were instructed to tell shoppers how many reward points they had and then to invite customers to use their points. American Express believed that Plenti members would be pleasantly surprised at how many points they had accumulated from the many retailers in the Plenti program. Cashiers would create a sense of delight in customers who might unexpectedly receive $25 or $50 off a purchase. Prior to the Plenti launch, American Express asked me to help them understand the neuroscience of unexpected rewards to ensure customers loved the program.

American Express's idea that unexpected savings build loyalty had merit. In 2012, newly hired JCPenney CEO Ron Johnson overhauled the pricing strategy of this legacy retailer by eliminating coupons and instituting "fair and square" everyday prices. Johnson was famous as the Apple executive who designed and launched their retail stores and invented the Genius Bar. Prior to Apple, he was head of merchandising at Target and had redesigned the stores to have a young, hip vibe. Johnson was expected to lead a turnaround at tired and dusty JCPenney, a company that saw annual revenue peak in 2008 at nearly $20 billion, sliding by over two-thirds to $6.7 billion in 2021.

Here's the coupon dilemma Johnson faced: in the US, $300 billion of physical coupons are distributed, but less than 1% are redeemed. JCPenney could save millions if they stopped printing and mailing coupons. Johnson said, "I thought people were just tired of coupons and all this stuff." Investors agreed. When Johnson announced the changes he planned to make, JCPenney's stock rose 24%.

Eliminating coupons produced an immediate backlash. A bring-back-coupons revolution erupted as customers boycotted JCPenney, sending revenues into a tailspin. Johnson grossly misunderstood JCPenney's core customers and was fired after fourteen months. Surveys showed that JCPenney's shoppers enjoyed seeing the printout showing "how much you saved today" on their receipts. *Time* magazine wrote that Johnson "immediately rejected everything existing customers believed about the chain and stuffed it in their faces."

Previous moves to eliminate coupons have produced similarly strong responses. In 1995, General Mills instituted "everyday low prices" in lieu of coupons for their breakfast cereals. After other manufacturers failed to follow suit, they quickly resumed issuing coupons. The following year, the world's largest advertiser, Procter & Gamble, and nine other consumer product manufacturers decided to stop issuing coupons. They reasoned that since so few coupons were redeemed, eliminating coupons would save money. "There's nothing effective about a system that fails 98 percent of the time," said P&G spokesperson Elizabeth Moore. Consumers, however, saw the situation differently and boycotted products from P&G. Soon thereafter, P&G coupons reappeared.

Even though redemption rates are low, coupon use, especially of digital coupons, continues to grow. Over one-half of US adults, 100 million people, have redeemed a digital coupon. If people use coupons simply to save money, the increase in household incomes in the last several decades should have reduced their use since it takes time to find coupons and clip or print them. But the data show otherwise. Before studying the Plenti program, my group ran a smaller-scale experiment to see what coupons do to the brain.

We gave ninety people seventy dollars to spend while shopping online in my lab. One-half of the participants got an unexpected pop-up coupon worth $10 while shopping, and the other half did not. When this study was performed, we had not yet developed the technology to measure neurologic Immersion using wireless devices, so we measured the neurochemical signals that make up Immersion by taking blood samples before and after people shopped.

We found that those who received a coupon had a 14% increase in oxytocin and an 8% decrease in the attention marker ACTH. This caused a 4% decrease in participants' heart rates while shopping and a 90% increase in vagus nerve activity. The brains of participants in the control group who did not receive a coupon did not produce these physiologic responses.

The increase in oxytocin is particularly interesting. It indicates that the brain processes unexpected rewards similarly to the way it would process being handed money by a human being. The bump in oxytocin makes people relaxed and happy. In fact, participants' happiness after shopping increased in lockstep with the change in oxytocin: the more oxytocin a participant's brain released, the more he or she enjoyed the experience. Coupons are used not only to save money; they also make shopping more enjoyable.

We used a similar approach to see what American Express's Plenti program did to shoppers' brains. We built a store in our lab that included personal care products, cleaning supplies, Pop Tarts, pasta, Doritos, and other common items. A bubbly graduate student named Adriana was the cashier, and 103 participants were recruited and given a $30 American Express gift card (naturally) and were asked to fill a shopping basket. We used blood draws before and after shopping to measure oxytocin and attention. Participants were randomly assigned to either a baseline condition, in which they checked out of the store while Adriana thanked them for shopping, or a reward condition where Adriana told them that they had received an unexpected Plenti reward. American Express forecasted that the average Plenti client would earn $40 annually, so this is what participants in the reward condition received during checkout.

The analysis showed that Plenti rewards spiked oxytocin by 67% and reduced ACTH by 3%. Neither biomarker changed in the no-reward condition, just as in our prior study. And, similar to that experiment, Plenti rewards produced a 14% increase in happiness compared to participants' average pre-shopping baseline. There was no change in happiness for those who did not receive a reward. As we predicted, given the ease of recall for emotional experiences, participants who were surveyed a week after they shopped reported that their happiness after shopping was 20% higher—but only if they had received a Plenti reward. Rewarded shoppers were 19% more likely to be loyal to the store compared to the unrewarded, saying they would come back for another shopping study, even with blood draws. This loyalty effect was persistent—a week after the study, we found the same degree of loyalty for rewarded participants. Those in the no-reward group were not interested in having us torture them again.

These findings were primarily due to reactions by women. Compared to men, the change in oxytocin in women who received rewards was 100% higher. As a result, women who received rewards reported nearly 400% more happiness after shopping compared to men. This helps explain why women spend one hundred more hours per year shopping than do men. We might dismiss "retail therapy" as a myth, but if shopping comes with unexpected rewards, then this study proves it has salubrious physiologic effects. Loyalty rewards and coupons substantially enhance the shopping experience.

Ron Johnson must have known, but dismissed, data showing that the majority of JCPenney's customers are female. Just like with Plenti rewards, the results of the coupon study were primarily due to women's responses. By eliminating coupons at JCPenney, Johnson took the fun out of shopping for precisely those who enjoyed it the most.

There is an unhappy conclusion to this story: in July 2018, American Express shuttered the Plenti program. I felt like I had a stake in Plenti's success, and I regularly shop at retailers in the Plenti consortium, including Rite Aid and Macy's. In the two years during which I was a member of the Plenti program, never did a cashier say to me, "You have Plenti points. Would you like to use them?" A rewards recitation is absolutely necessary in a loyalty program.

The casual restaurant chain Panera Bread runs one of my favorite loyalty programs. I eat at Panera regularly and about every other visit the cashier tells me that I have earned a free drink or cookie, at which point I get that unexpected oxytocin burst. I'm a loyal Panera customer because I enjoy their healthy food but also because I'm rewarded at their stores. American Express was unable to train and motivate the multiple retailers in the Plenti program to make unexpected rewards neurologically valuable by sharing them with shoppers. Loyalty programs can work, and work better if cashiers mention rewards. And hiring an Adriana who will do this with enthusiasm will strengthen the effect.

## WHERE TO SHOP

How do you choose where to shop? For most people, convenience is essential, as are prices, variety, and service. Among these, service is the most important to customer loyalty. Yet increasingly, what a company stands for and how they treat stakeholders also matter. Younger people get credit for being the most concerned about the values of companies they patronize—70% of millennials say they consider a company's values before making a purchase. Across all age groups, nearly half of consumers report that a company's values affect where they shop. Values violations can undermine the loyalty of consumers who companies work hard to maintain. Sometimes business leaders try to make up for these violations through apologies.

In 2007 Facebook launched a feature called Beacon. Beacon allowed Facebook to track members' internet usage at all times unless they explicitly opted out. The overreach of Beacon caused a rapid and virulent backlash among Facebook members and nonmembers. People claimed that Facebook was spying on them in order to monetize non-Facebook online activities. As a "Drop Facebook" campaign gained momentum, Facebook's founder and CEO, Mark Zuckerberg, issued an apology, saying, "We've made a lot of mistakes building this feature, but...we were excited about Beacon because we believe a lot of information people want to share isn't on Facebook." But the Zuck's apology had little effect: criticism mushroomed until Beacon was removed. After the kerfuffle subsided, Facebook's stock price and revenue rebounded.

When Ron Johnson resigned as CEO of JCPenney, he told his board, "If you wanna go back to the old business model, the sooner you do that the better." It wasn't really an apology for his strategic failures; it was more like the obnoxious bully Nelson Muntz in *The Simpsons* departing by saying, "Smell you later."

British Petroleum (BP) was responsible for a mistake that had very different results. In 2010, BP was operating the oil rig Deepwater Horizon, which exploded and caused a massive oil spill in the Gulf of Mexico. BP's CEO, Tony Hayward, issued an apology immediately after the accident, saying, "We're sorry for the massive disruption it's caused... There's no one who wants this over more than I do. I'd like my life back." His self-absorption after eleven men lost their lives in the accident, mothers lost sons, and children lost fathers did not sit well with the public. Although Hayward accepted responsibility for the spill and pledged that BP would repair the damage, commentators and much of the public believed his apology lacked sincerity and regret. Hayward was forced to resign a few weeks after the incident due in part to his feeble apology. A month after the oil spill, BP's market capitalization had dropped in half, losing $105 billion in value.

Here's the problem with apologies for actions that violate a company's values: many seemingly contrite CEOs are aware that the mistakes they are apologizing for cannot be corrected or will not be corrected in a timely manner. Yet they pledge to make amends in their apologies anyway. So how are consumers to know if apologies are sincere or not? People have to rely on an imperfect measurement technology to make this call: their own impressions and the impressions of others, including potentially more informed opinions in news reports. The fracturing of news media has led to a decline in investigative journalism, so consumers must increasingly develop their own opinions about businesses. Most of what one reads in the news has a spin on it, and has often been crafted by public relations professionals.

So, how do companies maintain customer loyalty in the face of disasters?

In order to find out, we asked study participants to watch videos of eight apologies by corporate CEOs that had come to the public's attention. The corporations included United Airlines (poor integration of services after purchasing Continental airlines), Sony (PlayStation network outage), Domino's Pizza (video of employees putting dirty ingredients into food), Barilla pasta (CEO stating he is homophobic), Eurostar (trains repeatedly breaking down), Whole Foods (overpricing), Toyota (unexpected engine surges), and Volkswagen (falsifying diesel engine emissions data). One-half of the problems were corrected within a year of the apology (United Airlines, Sony, Domino's Pizza, and Barilla), while the other companies did not correct the issue (Eurostar, Whole Foods, Toyota, and Volkswagen).

Study participants were paid $3 for each video they watched. Immediately after the video, they could wager some or all of their earnings on whether the mistake was resolved. If they were correct, they would double their money, but if they were wrong, they would lose what they had bet. This approach incentivized participants to pay attention to the apologies and analyze them for any clues that might indicate that the CEO was sincere or was lying. My team checked newspaper accounts of post-apology actions to determine whether the violation had been corrected or not. Our analysis would thus be a statistical horse race. Which was more accurate, people's conscious impressions and wagers or their unconscious brain activity?

Using their intuition, participants were no better than chance at identifying the companies that had fixed problems. Ditto for consciously chosen wagers—the bets did not predict which

CEOs were sincere. This inability to identify sincere apologies might be because some of the speeches were written by public relations firms that had rehearsed the CEOs so they would seem sincere. We hypothesized that even with this preparation, people's brains could identify which problems had been fixed.

That's just what we found. A combination of neurologic signals associated with Immersion identified sincere apologies with 61.3% accuracy, a value that is statistically greater than the 50% accuracy one would get by randomly guessing. CEOs whose companies actually fixed the violation generated more Immersion in viewers than insincere CEOs. People's unconscious emotional reactions to apologies were informative, while their conscious appraisal of the apologies were not.

The neurologic data revealed what makes an apology believable. First, the CEO has to address the audience directly and identify the problem in the opening statement. Next, using concrete language, he or she should describe how the company will remedy the problem. Finally, our analysis shows that sincere apologies clearly state how the company will minimize the harm done. Clear, specific, and actionable statements produce high emotional resonance rather than the nagging sense that the wool is being pulled over one's eyes.

The data establish that sincere apologies are immersive because CEOs are confident that the problem is being fixed. Some CEOs might be able to fake it, but we all have "tells" that reveal the truth. In this case, the "tells" are recognized unconsciously, but they are there nonetheless. It is better for CEOs to wait a few days, assess the problem, and create a plan to fix it before going on camera and hoping they can improvise sincerity. The best way for a CEO to make a sincere apology is to actually solve the problem—go figure. This is also the way to save that nice CEO job and maintain customer loyalty even when bad things happen.

## EXTRAORDINARY EXPERIENCES

My youngest daughter, Elke, and I have traveled the world together. Every spring, she picks some place in the world and we go there for a week's adventure. We have been to Japan, Brazil, England, Italy, and throughout the US. During a train ride from London to Salisbury on our way to see Stonehenge, we started discussing great meals. I was able to tick off many of my favorites. They were in Amsterdam (Oceana), Copenhagen (Stud!o, Høst), New York (The Lambs Club), London (The Wolseley), Cartagena (Casa Pestagua), and a few other cities. As I described why I was in these exotic locations and with whom I'd dined, my daughter said, "I don't think it was just the food; I think it was the people and the place." Smart girl. She's probably right about the setting affecting how much I enjoyed the meal. I decided to put her hypothesis to the test.

Elke, then aged sixteen, and I wore fitness sensors with the Immersion app installed while we ate dinner at two restaurants. The first would establish a baseline. We used my family's everyday favorite, Panera Bread. Elke and I spent fifty-four minutes at Panera and enjoyed the food and service. Average Immersion during the meal was 9% greater than the live-experience benchmark. Peak Immersion was 100% over benchmark and frustration was 34% higher than the benchmark. Panera served us tasty food, provided good service, and created a positive experience for us. The data showed that Elke was 9% more immersed while dining at Panera than I was. She had chosen the location, and her data reflected that.

Our comparison restaurant was a curated dining experience called Opaque—a spot known for "Dining in the Dark" in Santa Monica, California. A blind Swiss reverend named Jorge Spielmann concocted the idea to serve dinner in complete darkness. In 1999, Spielmann opened the Blindekuh (Blind Man's Bluff) restaurant in Zurich after friends who dined blindfolded at his home said it enhanced their enjoyment of the food. Opaque is the US incarnation of the Blindekuh dining experience, which was specifically designed to be immersive. And really dark.

Floating. That was how it feels to sit in a room in which there is not a pinprick of light. I could feel the table with my hands and the chair with my legs, but I was unable to orient myself after a sight-impaired server named Rafael led my daughter and me, hand-on-shoulder, through the darkest dark I've ever experienced.

Rafael asked me to remove my watch because its face glowed. Occasionally, we would see tiny flashes of light that we found moderately disconcerting. Elke discovered that the flashes were static electricity sparking from our hands as we moved them across the black tablecloth feeling our way toward the food.

This was my second time eating at Opaque and Elke's first, and she was anxious about being in a completely dark setting. Stress inhibits Immersion, and I made a mental note to analyze her psychological safety when I reviewed the data. The meal had five items: an amuse-bouche, an appetizer, a palate cleanser, a main course, and a dessert. The content of each course was a surprise. After we ate it, Rafael asked us what we thought we had eaten. We usually guessed wrong, and then he told us what we had really had. All courses were intricately prepared with unexpected ingredients.

The data confirmed Reverend Spielmann's observation that dark dining is immersive, especially the first time. We were at Opaque for one hour and forty-five minutes (time moves slowly in the dark), and Elke's average Immersion was three standard deviations above the Immersion benchmark value. Her peak Immersion and her frustration were nearly identical to those at Panera Bread, with most of her frustration occurring in the first twenty minutes of the experience. The data on psychological safety showed that she quickly got over her fear of being in complete darkness. Overall, though, Elke was just 3% more immersed at Opaque than at Panera Bread.

My visit to Opaque—my second time there—differed from Elke's. My average Immersion was right at the benchmark value. A good experience, but not nearly as immersive as Elke's. Like Elke, when eating at Opaque I doubled the benchmark for peak Immersion and experienced frustration 33% more than the frustration benchmark. The immersive parts of the meal were fabulous for me, and the rest of it was okay. Opaque has a $99 per person prix fixe menu, so with tip I dropped $240 for the two of us. Averaging Immersion for Elke and me, eating at Opaque was 2% more immersive than eating at Panera Bread, and dinner for two at Panera was just $40. At Opaque, it cost me about $30 to get one unit of Immersion, while at Panera it only cost $5 per unit. Panera wins by being a more cost-effective way to have an immersive dining experience. On the other hand, Elke's two-hour experience at Opaque induced extended periods of peak Immersion, something that is extraordinarily rare.

My recommendation from this mini-study is that you should treat yourself to an extraordinary experience like Opaque once in a while because deep Immersion is so valued by the brain; the rest of the time, eat at Panera. Retailers that can create multisensory experiences like Opaque have a greater chance of generating emotional responses. At Opaque, Rafael told us stories about his life and about the amazing food we were eating. Narrative retailing can do the same thing, building an emotional story that enhances the customer journey. The story should not only be visual, as it was in the phone store, but it can also be branded by adding something proprietary. For example, Four Seasons Hotels and Abercrombie & Fitch brand their customer experiences with unique scents. Neurologic Immersion due to smell alone can vary by an order of magnitude, effectively jump-starting an emotional connection. Think how happy you are walking by a Subway sandwich shop when you inhale the smell of baking bread; popcorn carts at Disney properties similarly pump out smells to attract customers. Retailers can add upbeat music and plenty of things to touch to engage all five senses.

An American manufacturer of sport utility vehicles offered qualified buyers a chance to drive an off-road course while being coached by a professional driver. The driver wore a smartwatch that sent data to cloud servers through a mobile app to measure Immersion. The data showed that people were deeply immersed in the most challenging parts of the course.

Experiential selling like this is most effective when the demo ends on an Immersion peak. This is when the associate should close the sale. This "wow" factor is why high-adrenaline experiences like skydiving or go-kart racing offer customers a subscription for future use immediately after the experience concludes. Sales should be closed in public because seeing others make a purchase offers social proof that the product or service is valuable.

Offering customers a coffee or another aromatic drink while they shop is another initiator of sensual generosity. My daughter Alex and I experienced this in the historical but tiny town of Delphi on the slopes of Mount Parnassus in Greece. Chilled from the snow, we tucked into an antique shop scented with incense and old rugs. As classical Greek music played, the proprietor offered me a glass of a licorice-flavored drink called ouzo. As we started talking, I started shopping, and—voilà!—I purchased a Greek orthodox icon. That icon hangs in my office, and I get a burst of enjoyment when I look at it because the experience of buying it activated all my senses.

## EXPENSIVE PURCHASES

Large purchases can generate conflict between couples. Cars, houses, and even vacations can be stress-inducing. A survey by Zillow found that 70% of couples argue when buying or selling a home. I wondered if measuring Immersion in couples would reduce conflict during large purchases by giving them objective data on not only their own preferences, but on their partner's. A TV production company thought the neuroscience of house-hunting might make an interesting show, and they fronted money to film a pilot.

In the show, we saw Greg and his wife hunting for a house in Denver. Cameras followed them while I watched their Immersion data on my laptop. In the first house they visited, Amy's Immersion in every room was well above the average and peaked continually. Her continuously high Immersion advertised her personality as agreeable and empathic. Amy's desire to get along with others might have inhibited her from telling Greg her preferences as they house-shopped. Watching Amy, I could also see she was an introvert, while Greg was an extrovert.

As they walked through the first of three houses they would tour, Amy and Greg both said they liked it and would consider purchasing it. The first house was older and would need extensive remodeling. Examining their Immersion data room by room told a different story: their data showed the potential for conflict. What Amy liked in the house Greg did not care about, and vice versa. Amy loved the family room, while Greg loved the garage; Greg loved the big yard, and Amy loved the nursery.

Their neurologic responses to the second house had the opposite pattern. Amy's and Greg's Immersion data surged at the same times. Even better, their average Immersion for this house was higher than for the first house. This finding, together with a reduction in conflict because their Immersion data moved together, put it ahead of house number one.

My ability to advise Amy and Greg on which house to buy hit a roadblock when I saw the data from the third house. Averaging Amy's and Greg's Immersion for this house showed that it was higher than for the other houses. Digging into the data, I found that the high average was due to Greg; he adored this house. Unfortunately, this house produced the lowest Immersion for Amy among the three houses she toured. Compounding this split decision, Greg's and Amy's Immersion while walking through the house were unrelated, showing that each was indifferent about the features the other person valued.

It was time to debrief Greg and Amy. As the cameras rolled, I asked Amy what it was about the first house that produced such a powerful effect on her. That's when the tears started. Amy told me that the house reminded her of the home she grew up in, the home her father had just put up for sale. He was selling it because Amy's mother had passed away two weeks ago. The data showed that Amy had a powerful emotional response. Amy did not discuss her emotional reaction with Greg when they walked through the house, but the data revealed her true feelings. I asked the director to turn off the cameras while I apologized for upsetting Amy. I hugged her, and we took five while she collected herself.

Once the cameras started rolling again, I explained that the second house had high average Immersion and was less likely to cause conflict. They both liked the same things in the house, and what they both disliked could be remodeled. Amy and Greg said the second house would work for them and they were ready to make a purchase. I advised them to get a good night's sleep before making their decision. The brain consolidates information by building associations during sleep. Amy's highly emotional state was not the time to make an important financial decision.

Retailers of high-end products, investment advisors, and

others asking people to make substantial financial decisions should think not only about what will satisfy needs, but how a purchase might produce conflict between couples. Conflict is mitigated when the sales associate makes an emotional connection with all of those involved in the decision. Look for facial expressions or body language to see if a person is stressed or unhappy and address them directly. If one party to a transaction is not talking, ask him or her for input. Think of a "sweetener" that can help engage the dissatisfied party to get him or her on board with the purchase. If a purchase decision produces conflict between the buyers, the sale is likely to fall apart, so the sales associate should address options up front so conflict does not fester.

## DISNEYLAND REDUX

Several years ago, a guy I'd never met invited me to go to Disneyland with him. The guy was journalist Charles Montgomery, and he was writing a book on happiness. He wanted me to give him a play-by-play on what made Disneyland so immersive. Charles is Canadian and had never been to Disneyland.

We concocted a number of experiments to do during our visit. For example, Charles brought an empty wallet that I pretended to drop. Every time I dropped it, and no matter how fast I walked away, someone ran after me to return it. I purposely bumped into people and every one of them apologized to me. When people are having an extraordinary experience, they enjoy themselves, treat others well, and spend freely. That's the fully immersive experience economy.

Customer experience designers should plan, rehearse, and

improve every aspect of the customer journey. Most designers focus on the physical experience, but I recommend augmenting this with the approach used by director Alfred Hitchcock. For every movie he directed, he had two scripts, a blue one and a green one. The blue script had the lines the actors would speak and the set directions. The green script specified the emotions Hitchcock wanted the audience to feel. Retailers already use blue scripts. The experience economy demands that these are complemented with green scripts in order to create immersive and enjoyable experiences that customers will return to repeatedly.

Employees are the ones who create great experiences, and it is to them that we turn next.

## KEY TAKEAWAYS

1. Create a multisensory narrative for customers.
2. Plan surprises during the customer journey to spike Immersion.
3. Move customers toward higher-profit-margin purchases during their journey.
4. Use information technology to customize experiences at scale for each customer.
5. Demonstrate social proof to introduce new products and services.

# CHAPTER 6

# BUILDING HIGH-PERFORMANCE ORGANIZATIONS

I had to say no. I'm 6'4" and weigh 200 pounds. Even wearing a blow-up sumo wrestling suit, I was afraid I would crush the skinny folks waiting in line to get into the ring at the Las Vegas headquarters of Zappos. It was an experience designed to make Zapponians happier at work.

Why don't all workplaces strive to make work an adventure? Let's be honest; for many people, work sucks. The polite term for sucky work in economics is that labor generates "disutility." This persistent idea in economics has its roots in the philosophy of Plato and Aristotle. These thinkers lived in economies in which manual labor was done by slaves while enlightened men (and just a few women) enjoyed the leisure to perambulate and philosophize. Even the word *labor* conjures fatigue-inducing physical exertion that still constitutes work for many of the planet's inhabitants. Yet we can still ask the question: why isn't your job making you happy?

As I write this, the US unemployment rate is at a 50-year low of 3.6%. More than 155 million American are working; that is fully 44% of all men, women, and children living in the country. The shortage of employees has created production bottlenecks. Companies are digging deep to overcome this, pulling former employees out of retirement to fill rosters. Goldman Sachs created a program called "Returnship" that puts mature hires through a ten-week training and mentoring program so they can reenter the workplace with appropriate skills.

There are similar labor shortages throughout the developed and developing world where sustained economic growth and low fertility have maxed out the labor force. Switzerland's unemployment rate is 2.3%, Japan's is 2.4%, the Czech Republic's is 2.6%, Germany's is 3.2%, Denmark's is 3.7%, the UK's is 3.8%, and Mexico's is 3.5%. As Christopher Bishop, head of the Herman Miller Innovation Lab has said, "The war of talent is over. Talent has won."

Companies face the binding dilemma of simply keeping their offices and factories running. Here is another way to think about this problem: how do companies keep their highest-performing employees from going to work elsewhere?

Cash is the simplistic answer. The tight labor market has driven up wages. But it turns out that people acclimate to higher salaries quickly and then move to a new company to get the next raise. Are there other margins that impact where and how people choose to devote their effort and expertise? There are in fact several, including alignment with the organization's purpose and trust between work colleagues.

Workplace culture has substantial effects on productivity. Research by my lab and others has shown that—surprise!— people put in more effort when doing jobs they enjoy. *Job crafting* is the term of art for work responsibilities that align by design with an employee's interests and strengths. But now we face that same old bugaboo: asking people what they most enjoy doing at work. I have spent countless hours talking to employees, from entry-level new hires to seasoned executives, seeking to ascertain what they enjoy most about their jobs. In response, people hem and haw. I spoke to a senior executive at a multibillion-dollar software company who, after receiving coaching to prepare her for a promotion, realized that she would rather coach others than accept the promotion. She left her employer and revamped her career to do exactly that. But she did not know in advance that she enjoyed coaching because she had not experienced it. Just as asking someone how much they "like" a movie or advertisement poorly predicts outcomes, it is difficult to assess the parts of one's job that are satisfying.

In my previous book, *Trust Factor: The Science of Creating High-Performance Companies*, I discussed the neuroscience of workplace culture and how to measure and improve it. I also developed software that organizations use to build trust and improve alignment with their purpose. This chapter complements my earlier findings by showing how to build high-performance cultures through the lens of Immersion.

## NEURAL JOB CRAFTING

Measuring psychological safety and Immersion while people work is the most direct way to create the conditions for high performance and match strengths with tasks. I call this "neural job crafting." By measuring what immerses people's brains at work and what produces frustration, employers can match each individual with tasks they love doing, ensuring performance at the highest level. Neural job crafting is like sports: if you played each of the nine positions in baseball, a coach could evaluate how effectively you performed in each position. Sports are easier to evaluate than work because in sports each player has just a few tasks and the production of each is observable. Most people at work are doing multiple tasks, and productivity for many of them can be difficult to evaluate. This is why technology that maps neural activity into work tasks is so useful. People simply devote more discretionary effort to tasks they love doing. This is just human nature.

My team created an app that sent a text message to employees' phones once a threshold of Immersion or frustration had been met while they were working. Employees got four to five text messages a day, asking them to identify, using a drop-down menu, what they were doing. They could also fill in what they were doing using an open-ended "Other" space. Over the course of a month or more, this technique builds an objective portfolio of tasks that someone "loves to do" and others that they would "rather not do." These data change the conversation between an employee and his or her supervisor from what one must do to what one is best at doing.

My approach is similar to the experience sampling method (ESM) developed by my colleague Mihaly (Mike) Csikszentmihalyi in the 1970s. Mike and his colleagues randomly sent messages to pagers asking participants to report what they were doing and to offer a subjective rating of their moods. Csikszentmihalyi used these data to identify the relationship between what people do and how they feel. Most of the variation in moods and "flow," the sense of being lost in a task, have been shown to be due to the task itself rather than one's personality.

My approach, using a neurologic trigger rather than random messages, captures data from the most important parts of people's workday and avoids the self-report bias of a survey. This is the frontier of organizational development. My team has not collected enough data to prove that neural job crafting improves job satisfaction and organizational performance, but numerous reliable studies have shown that employees empowered with autonomy to work on what they love are substantially happier and more productive. Equally important, the organizations that promote employee autonomy are highly profitable.

The culture at Zappos effectively balances comradery, connection, and autonomy. Zapponians can spend as much time as they like on the phone with customers and can even connect them to other companies who might better fulfill their needs. The longest call to date was nearly eleven hours. The point of long customer service calls is not to sell more, but to make an authentic Personal Emotional Connection. Customer service, not shoes and clothing, is Zappos's main product.

The neural substrate of PEC is Immersion and, as we discussed in Chapter 5, Immersion is contagious. It travels from a customer service agent on the phone to a customer on the other end. In the same way that immersive stories are persuasive, the contagion of Immersion is also persuasive. Was the eleven-hour call worth it? Customer lifetime value at Zappos is extraordinarily high. Half of Zappos's customers return to make future purchases, and fully 75% of their revenue is due to repeat customers. This can only occur when Zappos's employees have the motivation and autonomy to immerse customers in the shopping experience. Eighty-two percent of Zapponians say it is a great place to work compared to 59% at a typical US company. Turnover is miniscule and the happiness is palpable, both inside and out of the sumo ring.

## FINDING STRENGTHS

The most common way to assess job fit is to discover what one is good at doing. This is a reasonable approach to job crafting because the brain obtains value when performing tasks with mastery. Various surveys seek to assess one's strengths by mapping personality dimensions onto work tasks. These surveys, and books about them, are bestsellers year after year because they help match people to jobs. Work not only involves physical and cognitive effort; it requires emotional labor. The effort required to perform at one's best is lower when job tasks align with innate and learned strengths.

The assessment of character strengths has its roots in the positive psychology movement that started in the 1990s. Research by professors Chris Peterson and Martin Seligman showed that there are six primary character strengths: wisdom and knowledge, courage, humanity, justice, temperance, and transcendence. Each primary strength can be decomposed into subsidiary strengths, providing survey-takers with insights they may not be aware of. The Gallup company distributes a strengths-finder survey that measures thirty-four character strengths that include harmony, ideation, competition, and focus. Each office at Gallup's Irvine, California, headquarters has a placard showing an employee's top two strengths. This signals what aspects of work are of most interest to that employee and is an effective way to improve communication and teamwork.

When people are able to exercise their strengths at work, they are more productive and more satisfied with their jobs. They even help colleagues more often. Being satisfied at work contributes to people's overall life satisfaction. Yet we still do not understand why, after millions of people have taken character strength surveys, everyone is not productive and happy at work.

## PSYCHOLOGICAL SAFETY

Certainly the fit of one's strengths to job duties is important, but this is only a small part of what it takes to have a productive and happy workforce. Let's dig into this by analyzing why people quit their jobs. Every year, about half the people who voluntarily quit have been in their jobs for less than twelve months. Money matters, especially in tight job markets with plenty of opportunities, as does career advancement. But most research shows that organizational frictions, especially with supervisors, are the primary reason people leave their jobs. We're back to "work sucks." One solution for this is better training of team members and supervisors in people skills using the techniques discussed in Chapter 4.

As you can imagine, companies spend piles of money to understand how supervisors affect teamwork. Google's Project Oxygen found that managers have substantial effects on team productivity. Great managers are servant leaders, coaching their direct reports toward success without micromanaging them. They communicate plans clearly but are also good listeners. My own research has shown that leaders who ask for help by saying "please" rather than making demands and who remember to thank colleagues for their efforts have more productive teams and have greater job satisfaction. Being nice matters because everyone wants to be respected. Google took the next step with Project Aristotle, discovering that the most effective teams are those with high psychological safety based on a self-report survey. Teams high in psychological safety trust each other implicitly and work effectively like a superorganism or jazz ensemble.

The Google research has convinced many companies that managers who coach colleagues toward goals in an environment of psychological safety will have stellar performance. But knowing and doing are quite different. How often can one survey employees and collect reliable data? Are employees of diverse backgrounds equally willing to report their emotional states in a survey? As an alternative to surveys, the psychological safety app I developed is being used to help managers create the conditions for effective teamwork by collecting objective data without interrupting people's work. Putting these insights into practice is especially important now as more teams work remotely.

A global technology company that holds over 80,000 meetings a year was concerned during the two-year COVID lockdown that teamwork would degrade. They used the Immersion platform to passively measure psychological safety during remote meetings rather than asking employees to complete a survey that may or may not accurately report their emotional states. The second-by-second data showed that effective managers increased psychological safety over the course of a one-hour team meeting, while ineffective managers did the opposite. As we discussed in Chapter 4, you can think of psychological safety as available bandwidth in the brain. When psychological safety is high, people will participate in meetings and remember what was said. Meetings with low psychological safety induce fear, so employees want to escape rather than participate.

Managers can establish psychological safety by starting a meeting—whether in-person, remote, or hybrid—by taking time to have people check in with each other. Another approach is to ask attendees to close their eyes for two minutes to relax so they can focus on the information in the meeting. During the meeting, leaders need to slow down to make space for attendee questions and comments. Better to cover three agenda items that people understand and remember than to discuss six that no one remembers. As with training, presentations should be limited to twenty minutes or less. The data also show that making eye contact during meetings is an effective way to demonstrate care and connection.

Data from a town hall meeting revealed how fatigue inhibits psychological safety. The CEO and senior leadership made presentations during an eight-hour event. During the first two hours, psychological safety was high and so was Immersion. People were absorbing information and enjoying the experience. By 10:00 a.m., psychological safety began to flag and was quite low as lunch approached. The lunch break provided a small fillip to psychological safety, but by 2:00 p.m. it decreased every twenty minutes thereafter. The last hour of the town hall was reserved for questions for the leadership team. By then, employees were stressed and cranky and the questions reflected this.

Just as with training, shorter is better. The town hall meeting would have been more effective if it had been held for one hour a day across a week rather than eight hours in one day. Because we are adults, we think we can tough it out and stay engaged in meetings for hours, but the data show that the brain needs rest and recovery. Otherwise, only a modicum of information is effectively conveyed to attendees. When information is critical, the meeting must be kept very short so people are fully immersed. No preamble, no jokes. Establish psychological safety and then get to the meat of the matter. Tell people what they need to know, remind them what you said, and then dismiss them with a call to action to ensure the information sticks.

## OFFICE DESIGN

Employees can increasingly choose where and when to work. We know that effective teamwork requires psychological safety. What about Immersion during work? I collaborated with a major office designer to determine whether physical office layout affects Immersion.

Employees in a manufacturing company located in the US Midwest were instructed to work in teams in different office layouts. The first location we tested had curved three-foot-high partitions surrounding a low table and chairs and was the least open space. The second location was a partially open workspace with a low partition and a high table with chairs. The third location was the most open, having no partition, a high table and tall barstool chairs that were situated near a coffee bar. We measured neurophysiology as groups of four employees sought creative solutions to a task they had not seen before under time pressure.

Productivity was highest in the most open location and dropped when office spaces had walls. This occurred for two reasons. First, psychological safety was highest in the most open space. This freed up neural resources for ideation. A 1% increase in psychological safety raised perceived closeness to colleagues by 1%, showing how psychological safety allows people to sync up with each other. This was more likely in the most open space even though the noise level was 30% higher than in the other two locations. The second reason for higher productivity in the open space was that employees were more neurologically immersed in their work. Team productivity increased linearly with Immersion as highly immersed employees put in additional effort. At the same time, the most immersed participants enjoyed the difficult task we gave them.

The open office layout was also the most desired location, and employees felt like it provided the most privacy because it was so busy that eavesdropping was impossible. Our analysis uncovered what makes offices desirable: good lighting and air flow, a comfortable temperature, and beautiful furniture. Design matters. It matters not just for aesthetics, but also for Immersion, productivity, and job satisfaction.

## THE VALUE OF THE OFFICE

As COVID infections eased and employees returned to the office, the technology company continued to measure psychological safety in hybrid meetings. When I isolated the data from those attending in person compared to those attending remotely, psychological safety was higher for employees who attended meetings in the office. Baseline anxiety varies quite a bit across individuals, so it could be that those worried about COVID infections stayed at home longer than did the less anxious. But when I checked data from other companies I found the same pattern: colleagues in the office are, on average, objectively psychologically safer than those working at home. Measuring and managing psychological safety is vitally important if leaders seek to create an office environment that is so compelling that employees want to spend time there. Innovation and teamwork are more effective when people collaborate in person. Yet few companies want to force employees to come to the office every day when many have acclimated to working remotely.

Human beings need to congregate and socialize with others, and monkeys can tell us why. My lab ran an experiment in which we administered intranasal oxytocin to pairs of capuchin monkeys. This primate species, which has white fur on its face, shoulders, and arms and a black cap of fur on the crown of its head, is extremely social and intelligent. Compared to monkeys that were administered a placebo spray, capuchins who received oxytocin were so relaxed that they did not feel the need to huddle close to another monkey as they typically do. The oxytocin-dosed monkeys went about their business in a relaxed way and protested less when another monkey took food they had dropped. Oxytocin administration mimics the caring connection that social creatures, including capuchin monkeys and humans, can feel when they are in proximity to others.

The monkey research shows us that when colleagues treat each other with care and kindness, the office can serve as a social-emotional hub. This will entice people to spend more days on-site rather than working remotely. The first step in making the office attractive is to actively reduce the stress that comes from commuting and sitting close to others. Leaders need to start slow: request, but don't demand, that employees work in the office two or three days a week. Senior managers must be exemplars for office attendance, even after travel. On-site stress can also be mitigated by offering wellness programs that include meditation, yoga, and exercise classes. An intermediate solution is to reserve a coworking location for employees to use that reduces concerns about commutes while still congregating modest-sized groups.

Another way to make the office attractive is to offer food and alcohol. Both substances, the latter in moderation, increase connection by stimulating oxytocin release. Offering catered lunches during a short window causes people to eat together and converse. Use long picnic-style tables to facilitate conversations among people who may not know each other. Make things fun by having a Friday night pizza and beer get-together at the office or a nearby restaurant. Celebrate victories, even small ones, regularly with food and a party.

Research from Harvard Business School shows that Silicon Valley engineers who socialize at work the most are also the most productive. These connectors offered help and advice to others and also learned where to get help when they needed it. Proximity increases communication, and communication leads to cooperation, even when the stakes are high. Research from my lab demonstrated that even with $500 on the line, strangers who got to know each other cooperated 70% of the time rather than grabbing all the money for themselves when making decisions in private. Moreover, neurologic data accurately identified in advance the 30% who cheated their partners: they were physiologically stressed, knowing that what they were saying was a lie. Violating someone's trust damages working relationships and happens more frequently when people interact remotely rather than in person.

Research from my lab has shown that when people engage in group rituals, oxytocin is released and connection and cooperation follow. The effect is so blunt that the brain even identifies those outside the group as worthy of cooperation. Rituals rapidly connect new and historically underrepresented groups of employees to the team as a whole. Company traditions can be as simple as ringing a bell when one closes a sale. The design firm IDEO has a Wednesday afternoon tea with freshly baked pastries that brings everyone out of their offices. The Swedish have a tradition called *fika*, which is a coffee break with a snack mid-morning and mid-afternoon in a dedicated *fika* room. Swedish data show that slowing down work improves its efficiency and quality. I personally run monthly walking meetings as a ritual that stimulates new ideas by getting people moving and talking in different ways. You can influence people to return to the office by holding a weekly drawing that colleagues become eligible for after working in the office for five consecutive days. My lab has also shown that oxytocin increases gratitude toward others, motivating discretionary effort and increasing job satisfaction.

Drinking after work with colleagues has upsides and downsides. Employees who drink after work with team members earn 10% more money, all else being equal, than abstainers. This effect is particularly powerful in men; male employees who go to bars at least once a month earn an additional 7% on top of the 10% alcohol premium. William James, the father of modern psychology, wrote that "Alcohol [is]...the great exciter of the Yes function in man."

But if drinks are charged to the office, be sure to enforce limits. Research from my lab established that a blood-alcohol concentration of 0.05% increases selfishness by 32% compared to people who consumed nonalcoholic drinks. In fact, selfish behavior increased linearly as people consumed more alcohol. This study showed that alcohol decreased psychological safety and caused a deterioration in people's moods. While a drink or two after work is fine, moderate to high alcohol consumption makes people unhappy, uncooperative, and anxious. You've been to bars; you know this. Bad behavior when employees party together damages relationships, which can be difficult to repair. This is especially true for those in leadership roles.

Social creatures naturally follow leaders and mirror how they are treated. Leaders can create psychological safety by authentically connecting to colleagues. This is as simple as saying, "How can I be of service to you?" in conversation. Over time, this produces a cascade of helping behaviors between colleagues. Another effective leadership practice that increases psychological safety is starting meetings with "gratitudes" where colleagues are invited to thank others for helping them. Many successful leaders write thank-you cards by hand to recognize those who put in extraordinary effort. Hiring a career coach to help colleagues grow can make the office "sticky" as well. Companies like Zappos maintain high retention among younger staff by employing life coaches.

## DOGS RULE

Many companies permit and even encourage colleagues to bring their pets to work, typically dogs. I ran an experiment to see if dogs at work affected Immersion and productivity or were just distractions. As we discussed in Chapter 1, a key issue in neuroscience is getting the right baseline for comparison. Was having no dogs the right baseline or should it be some other animal? You guessed it: we ran a dogs versus cats study (and compared both of these to a no-animal condition).

Three of my graduate students brought in their friendly dogs for the study and another three brought their cats. We collected neurophysiologic data while 141 individuals played with a dog, a cat, or sat quietly for ten minutes. Good study design biases an experiment against finding an effect. By having people interact with an unfamiliar animal, we sought to identify the effect of interacting with any dog or cat at work, not just an animal one had already bonded to. After the pet interaction, groups of four people completed a group task in which they could either share money with others or work alone and leave the lab with more cash.

Experiments are funny. You never know what you are going to find, but you often see what you are supposed to see. Playing with a dog or cat had a highly variable effect on Immersion—except, that is, for participants who had lived with four or more pets in their lifetimes. When these "animal people" played with a new dog, they were immersed in the experience, and Immersion carried over and had a positive effect on cooperation. Dogs may very well be training us to cooperate because they are indiscriminately friendly. All work requires cooperation, which is why innovative companies allow dogs at work.

What about cat owners? Our data showed that the more cats one had owned, the less immersed people were and the less they cooperated. Cats are territorial loners and, in my view, only semi-domesticated. Few cats run to the door and wag their tails when one returns home. Cats at work? Nah, better skip that.

## THE BENEFITS OF REMOTE WORK

Most teams in the post-COVID world will include colleagues who work in the office and others who work remotely. Since we have discussed the disadvantages of remote work, we should examine the advantages as well. Primary among the advantages is the autonomy it gives employees over their work lives. Autonomy is strongly related to productivity and job satisfaction. Autonomy also facilitates job crafting, enabling employees to build on their strengths and master work tasks.

Mastery has a recognizable signature in the brain driven by a reduction in conscious responses and increased activity in brain regions that regulate automaticity. One team of neuroscientists described mastery as "cool and focused" brain activity. You have probably experienced the opposite when you have had an amazing game of golf, tennis, or bowling and start to consciously think about why you are doing so well.

Inevitably, your performance will deteriorate. Those who have mastered a task do it with less effort, find it more enjoyable, and consistently perform at a high level.

Experiments run in my lab have shown that Immersion during work is significantly higher for participants empowered with autonomy compared to those who are micromanaged. This is true both when people work alone and when they are part of a team, as long as goals are clearly set. Our analysis quantified the autonomy-productivity relationship: those given autonomy are 10% more productive for every hour they work. Using the 2019 median wage, a company employing 100 people would increase its annual revenue by $343,000 by creating a culture of autonomy. The freedom to choose how and when one works is simply easier when people work remotely.

Research from my group discovered a second benefit of autonomy. Not only did people put in more discretionary effort when empowered by autonomy, but they also had a 31% bump in happiness compared to their pre-work baseline. Work, for these people, does not suck. In this study, those in the non-autonomy condition had no change in happiness at all. The findings from this experiment were confirmed using a national sample of US working adults. The data showed that employees with greater autonomy worked harder, were happier, and were more likely to stay with their employer over the next year. Enjoyment at work builds on itself. Autonomous employees reach mastery rapidly by drawing on their personality strengths. Mastery is reached faster when more time is spent doing a task. Remote work eliminates commute time, interruptions, and long lunches, and makes it easier to skip unnecessary meetings. As a result, people who work from home put in, on average, an extra hour of work per day.

After mastery is achieved, the brain does something really interesting. It seeks novelty. Mastery without variation ceases to be challenging, so the brain has the resources to imagine and experiment with different ways of doing a task. Autonomy is the foundation for innovation, and remote employees can tap into this superpower. Think of Steve Jobs and Steve Wozniak working alone in a garage as they laid the foundation for Apple. The two Steves had the freedom to design the Apple computer as they saw fit. When autonomy is paired with Immersion while working, employees ideate, experiment, and improve. This is how innovative companies sustain profit margins and revenue growth. Just be sure to find time to form connections with remote employees by inquiring about their personal lives, not just work obligations. Even remote employees should be in the office for important meetings with team members and clients. A couple of days a month in the office is sufficient for many remote employees to sustain neurologic connections that improve teamwork and make it enjoyable. A blow-up sumo-suit event might even bring them in.

But should we seek to influence employees and customers? The next chapter explains how to ethically influence those around us.

## KEY TAKEAWAYS

1. The office serves as a social-emotional hub that improves communication and teamwork.

2. Open office layouts produce more psychological safety and Immersion than closed offices.
3. Autonomy is the neurologic foundation for mastery and job satisfaction.
4. Neural job crafting effectively matches employees to their highest-Immersion tasks.
5. Dogs at work increase cooperation and happiness.

# CHAPTER 7

# CHANGING PREFERENCES

The 2016 campaign for president of the United States was wild. Love him or hate him, Donald Trump changed the way candidates campaigned. Even days before the election, nearly every poll predicted that Hillary Clinton would win by a landslide. We're back to the problem with surveys and people reporting what they intend to do. I am apolitical, so I had no dog in the Trump versus Clinton race. But as a behavioral scientist I was fascinated by the passion and rancor of the campaign. So I ran a couple of experiments to decipher the Trump phenomenon.

The first study measured Immersion live during the Republican debate on January 14, 2016. The participants were self-identified Republicans who said they would vote in the presidential primary. The study was held in my lab in California, where many Republicans are called RINOs for "Republican in Name Only." This term was first used to disparage President Theodore Roosevelt and describes "buffet Republicans" who only support parts of the party platform and tend to be more liberal than party stalwarts. These folks are less likely to support a candidate based on party affiliation alone, so they were an interesting group to measure.

January is early in the election cycle, and seven candidates participated in the debate, including Donald Trump, Dr. Ben Carson, Florida senator Marco Rubio, former Florida governor Jeb Bush, Texas senator Ted Cruz, Ohio governor John Kasich, and New Jersey governor Chris Christie. Neurologic data showed that Mr. Trump produced the most Immersion in the assembled Republicans, 7% more on average than the second-most immersive candidate, Mr. Rubio, 15% more than Mr. Kasich, and down the line to 32% more than Mr. Christie. This measurement was made ten months before the general election, and the Bloomberg poll at that time reported Republican support for Mr. Trump at 43%, Mr. Rubio at 14%, and Mr. Cruz at 12%, lining up nicely with the Immersion data. Support for the others were in the single digits.

Still, I was skeptical. Trump refused to follow the debate rules and continually interrupted the other candidates, so perhaps the data were simply reflecting his antics. We had an opportunity to check the quality of the data on January 28 when another Republican debate was held but Mr. Trump announced he would not attend. The Immersion data showed that Mr. Rubio produced the strongest connection with voters, consistent with the previous study. Indeed, Mr. Rubio was 16% more immersive than Mr. Trump had been two weeks prior. As before, Mr. Kasich ranked next on Immersion. The consistency in Immersion told us that the data were valid.

But, of course, candidates cannot avoid each other. By April, all the candidates except Messrs. Trump, Cruz, and Rubio had dropped out of the race and Mr. Trump was eventually elected president.

It costs between $4 million and $6 million to host a presidential debate. Is anyone's mind actually changed by debates? We asked participants in both our studies to rank the candidates they preferred before and after the debates. Neither debate changed anyone's rankings.

This chapter answers a core question about extraordinary experiences: do they actually change people's preferences? If so, how is this done and how can it be done better? This also opens up an ethical issue: should marketers, educators, and movie producers be given the ability to change people's preferences?

## THE BRAIN BASIS FOR PERSUASION

As we discussed in Chapter 1, the brain is an imperfect cost-benefit calculator. Imperfect because if one is tired, stressed, hungry, angry, or standing next to a beautiful person of either sex, the brain processes information differently. The social influences on choice are particularly strong. Think of how many times you have been at a restaurant and, after reviewing the menu, you decide to order chicken. Then someone at the table orders a steak and suddenly you change your mind.

Many unconscious factors also affect behavior. In a famous study, psychologist Geoffrey Miller and colleagues showed that strippers earn more from lap dances when they are ovulating.

The extra income was only earned by women who did not use the birth control pill so that their precise ovulatory state was unknown to them. Of course, ovulation was hidden from the patrons as well. The neurochemicals of ovulation, principally estrogen and progesterone, appeared to have unconsciously influenced the sexiness of their dancing. Other research shows that in naturally cycling women, the pitch of their voices is higher when they are ovulating, unconsciously signaling to potential mates that they are young enough to reproduce.

There is a dirty secret in neuroscience: averages are not very meaningful. In nearly every experiment I have run in the last two decades, the variation in neural activity around the average is enormous. This neural diversity is due in part to the multiple feedback loops between brain regions that a single neuroscience measurement device poorly captures. To combat this, my lab measures a dozen or more neural signals simultaneously. The multiple-measurement approach shows that when different people are in the same experience, different parts of the brain and peripheral nervous system activate with different strengths and at different times. If one were to only use one technique, like an electroencephalogram (EEG) or functional magnetic resonance imaging (fMRI), to measure brain activity in an experiment, parallel processing and feedback loops are unlikely to be captured. One source of this diversity is the soup of around 200 neurochemicals that bathe the brain. Just like dancers whose behavior changed when they were ovulating, neurochemicals allow the brain to adapt to small variations in internal and external environments. This rapid adaptation is the primary reason the brain is an imperfect cost-benefit calculator and is, as we will see, why persuasion can be effective.

## ADOPTING NEW TECHNOLOGY AND SAVING THE ENVIRONMENT

Influencing people to use new technology is difficult. Early adopters of tech love trying new things, but my lab wanted to know what would persuade regular Joes to purchase a new software product.

We designed an experiment that measured neural responses while people navigated through a computerized maze. They could earn money if they got to the end of the maze in one minute or less, but most of the maze was "fogged out" so people could only see a couple of moves ahead of their present location. Participants could purchase an imperfect helper algorithm that would offer them advice, or they could navigate on their own. In order to see what influenced people to purchase the algorithm, we varied the information participants received about it. Some were told its accuracy, while others were told the proportion of previous individuals who had paid to use the algorithm.

Even a low level of social proof (54% of previous participants using the algorithm) was more persuasive than information on the algorithm's accuracy. The neurologic data showed that when there was no information about the algorithm, and when its accuracy was specified, people just assumed it would work. The absence of "algorithmovigilance" can be dangerous as when drivers assume that their driving-assist software does not need to be monitored. Conversely, when social proof affected adoption, people monitored the algorithm attentively and, as a result, completed more mazes. We even found an unexpected bonus: those who completed mazes with help from the algorithm thought the task was easier than those who struggled by themselves. The algorithm delivered an enjoyable experience.

These data enabled us to build a profile of the persuadable. Participants who said that they thought others are generally trustworthy were substantially influenced by social proof and were more than twice as likely to purchase the algorithm. We also found that women were influenced more by social proof than by the algorithm's accuracy and purchased the algorithm twice as often as men did.

This study gives us a few clues about persuasion. As in previous research, social proof is the most effective method of influence. Yet social proof is only effective when information comes from a trustworthy source. Trust can be established by identifying one's similarity with a comparison group, known as the "people like us" approach. If people like us are doing this, then I should do it too. Conversely, when the source is perceived as untrustworthy, the message will be ignored. Fake news, anyone?

We also found that small steps can lead to big wins. Participants who adopted the algorithm thought it was easy to finish mazes and earn money. They were more likely to use the algorithm again in the next round of the experiment. If we wanted to further influence people to use the algorithm, we could have rigged the study so that the first several times the algorithm was used the maze was always completed. This "winner effect" suppresses stress hormones and convinces people to continue doing what they are doing. Small wins extend the impact of influence.

Let's take on another topic for which persuasion is difficult:

climate change. In keeping with my mantra that actions speak louder than words, my team and I designed a study to see if we could persuade people to take action to help the environment. We asked participants to watch a set of videos produced by nonprofit organizations about environmental damage. One half of the videos were fact-based and the other half were story-based. Participants earned money for watching each video and could donate their earnings to the featured non-profit if they so chose, but did not have to. The compensation was modest, and participants had electrodes placed on their torso and fingers, making them moderately uncomfortable. This made the donation decision meaningful.

It will not surprise you that stories about climate change gen-erated twice the donations compared to the fact-filled videos. People were more immersed in stories than in facts, and this neurologic response predicted their donations. To test if we changed their preferences, we gave participants the opportu-nity to subscribe to the Greenpeace newsletter and to commit to take a follow-up survey in two weeks. Those in the story condition agreed to both of these twice as often as those in the fact group. Here's another behavioral measure we built in: people who watched a story about the environment cleaned up their desks as directed in written instructions at double the rate of those in the fact group. We also tested whether these results held up when the information was presented in a written brochure rather than in a video; it did.

The behavioral data indicated that we changed preferences for at least several weeks by having people take multiple actions that reinforced the message. This could lead to a permanent preference change if additional information was sent over the following weeks and months that asked participants to continue to take actions to protect the environment.

Repetition, as we discussed in Chapter 4, not only helps people remember information, but can solidify information in the brain, leading to a preference change. The technical term for this is *long-term potentiation* or LTP. This occurs when neurons in a circuit activate intensively and then repeat the process over and over. LTP is described as "neurons that fire together, wire together." This means that repeated activation strengthens connections in a neural circuit, increasing the likelihood that it will activate in the future. This is how you become proficient at a sport; at first it is difficult, but with enough practice it becomes enjoyable.

In order to change preferences about the environment or anything else, the information the brain receives must be immersive and must be repeated. This means content creators have to produce experiences that people want to revisit. Selling works the same way. Salespeople must often talk to prospects multiple times to close a sale. In business-to-business sales, only 3% of prospects are ready to buy at any time. Research by Microsoft reported that 80% of sales were preceded, on average, by four no's before the prospect said yes. Repetition is the bread and butter of sales. Add to this storytelling and social proof, and the likelihood of closing a sale shoots up.

## CHANGING POLITICAL PREFERENCES

When my lab runs experiments that administer a drug to participants, we collect as much data as possible while the drug is active so fewer people are exposed to the substance. I happened to be running an oxytocin administration study in 2007 during the campaign for US president. With assistance from my colleague Jennifer Merolla, who is a political scientist, we assessed people's political preferences and compared them to a control group that received a placebo.

At the time of the study, Republican George W. Bush was serving his second term as president and Democrats controlled Congress. Participants, all US citizens, were asked to rate how much they trusted political figures, including the president and candidates in the Democratic and Republican primaries who were prominent in the news. Our published research reported that oxytocin increased Democrats' trust in Republican politicians, but only among those who entered the study with low trust. For these folks, oxytocin bumped up their trust of people in general as well as for other-party politicians. Republicans' trust in Democratic politicians was unaffected by oxytocin administration.

Oxytocin is the neurochemical signature of social proof, telling the brain that information is reliable. But why only for Democrats? To find out, we ran an experiment during the 2011 campaign for US president, when politics was again in the news. At this time, President Obama's reelection was in doubt. Polls in August 2011 showed Mr. Obama, running as a Democrat, being defeated by Republican candidate Mitt Romney by two percentage points. At the time, Mr. Romney was tied in the polls with Texas governor Rick Perry for the Republican nomination and was ahead of Senator Ron Paul and Congressperson Michele Bachmann by two and four points, respectively.

To assess preferences directly, we asked participants to rate their "warmth" toward candidates on a one to one-hundred scale, an approach commonly used in political science. Only US citizens were able to participate, and this time we used a different drug: synthetic testosterone. An effective way to prove causation is to demonstrate that more than one physiologic challenge changes behavior. Testosterone is, roughly speaking, the anti-oxytocin. Findings from my lab and many others have documented that testosterone increases reactive aggression, selfishness, and confidence in one's abilities. Whether it affects political preferences had never been tested.

Taking blood samples at the start of the study, we found that Republicans and Democrats had identical testosterone levels. But when we segmented the sample by strength of party affiliation, the data showed that baseline testosterone in weakly affiliated Democrats was 19% higher than in strongly affiliated Democrats. Baseline testosterone in Republicans did not vary by the strength of party affiliation. Participants were tested again sixteen hours after testosterone treatment to give the drug time to get into the brain. When weakly affiliated Democrats received additional testosterone, their commitment to the Democratic party fell by 12% and they reported 45% warmer feelings toward Republican candidates for president. Testosterone did not affect preferences for strongly affiliated Democrats or strong or weak Republicans. The findings from both studies are consistent with research showing that, compared to Republicans, Democrats tend to be more open-minded and thus potentially more persuadable.

Political scientists call the preference change from Democrat to Republican a "red shift." Testosterone did not cause a red shift in everyone, just in Democrats who may have already been more open to Republican viewpoints as evidenced by their weak party affiliation. This group's high baseline testosterone may have also increased confidence in their own opinions rather than relying on what others think. Persuasion is likely when the target is already leaning in the direction of influence. You should not conclude from the oxytocin and testosterone administration studies that drugs are needed to change preferences. This approach was used to show the causal effect of neurochemicals on preferences, even ones thought to be quite stable like political preferences.

There are several practical applications of this research. For example, watching football games and boxing matches raises testosterone in men. Political ads shown during these broadcasts will have a better chance of changing the voting behavior of weakly affiliated male Democrats than running a commercial during a sitcom that is unlikely to affect testosterone. As we discussed above, women's preferences are also influenced by neurochemicals. Research has shown that women who are ovulating prefer more symmetric faces when assessing male romantic partners. Political ads that accentuate a male politician's facial symmetry might have more influence on ovulating female voters, especially if they are weakly affiliated Democrats. The lazy brain appears to confound the evaluation of romantic partners with the evaluation of those vying for leadership positions.

Persuasion can change preferences when the target of persuasion is physiologically and psychologically open to change, whether they know this or not, and when influence is focused on something of interest. The metabolically stingy brain is not interested in the set of all possible things a person might do, but in just a few things it needs immediately. Social creatures follow social signals.

Humans are persuadable because the considerable variation in brain activity means there is a range of neural states that open the imperfect cost-benefit calculator to persuasion. Grocery shopping while you are hungry is the obvious example, but so is shopping for a new car at the end of an exhausting workday when all your brain wants to do is shut down and rest. Tiredness suppresses the prefrontal cortex's typical inhibition to accept the first available option. That is how your neighbor ended up with a purple Nissan Cube with pink wheels. Or why you give in and buy your child who eats organic everything a McDonald's Happy Meal when he will not stop whining.

The remainder of this chapter will explain how to prompt the conditions in others' brains that increase the likelihood of persuasion. But before we do this, let's take a moment to ask if you *should* persuade others.

## THE ETHICS OF PERSUASION

Since the brain is metabolically lazy, it is difficult to have undue influence on neurologically healthy adults as persuasion requires considerable activity in the brain's executive center, the prefrontal cortex. Children, adults with cognitive impairments, and people under the influence of drugs or alcohol have diminished capacity and are more easily persuadable. Trying to influence these people is nearly always ethically wrong in my view, though many advertisements still target children. Adults are fair game as long as they have the ability to say no. For example, people need to be given enough time and a sufficient number of comparable options to make a decision that is in their best interest. If the dinner choices are liver or liver and onions, that is not much of a choice.

One of my best friends, Dr. C, is a psychiatrist who runs a large inpatient treatment center where the psychotic, delusional, demented, high on drugs, and suicidal are admitted. In these cases, he has argued, a physician must convince patients and their families to consent to a course of treatment that initially will be unpleasant. In other words, an effective psychiatrist must be paternalistic in that she or he restricts the choices a patient can make for the patient's own good. The patients are not of "right mind" and cannot make appropriate decisions for themselves. Patients' families, too, must be persuaded, and they have the right and ability to reject treatment options. British philosopher John Stuart Mill wrote that paternalism is only acceptable to prevent harm to others or oneself. This clearly applies to those with diminished capacity to choose.

Let's move in a bit from there. Suppose your uncle's spouse of forty years died and he is so depressed he wants to jump off a bridge. If he is of "right mind," should this be allowed? Most people would argue that we have an ethical obligation to try to convince a suicidal person not to kill himself. Pharmacotherapy can reduce suicidal ideation in hours to weeks, and for many people, this helps them through a period of intense anxiety and they return to generally happy lives. At the same time, some countries and some US states have legalized euthanasia if a person is judged by a psychiatrist to be cognitively intact. The doctor must determine whether the patient has the ability to weigh the consequences and make an informed choice. It is ethical to influence someone when they have the capacity to weigh options without coercion.

A study from my lab examined the ability of people to say no in a less dire situation. In nearly all experiments, study participants are required to consume all the content the investigator wants to understand. If the content is TV commercials, study volunteers watch the entire commercial while neural responses are measured. But in real life, most of us hover our mouses over the "skip" button while we wait for an ad to play before we can enjoy our chosen entertainment. I thought it would be important to understand the brain processes involved when people choose to stop watching content.

This experiment showed people videos from nonprofit organizations focused on alleviating social ills. Participants were informed that they could stop watching the videos at any time. Volunteers earned money just for starting a video, and there was no penalty for stopping. In fact, those who wanted to get paid and leave the lab quickly should have skipped every video after a few seconds. When participants stopped each video, whether it was at the beginning, middle, or end, a pop-up window offered them a choice to donate some of the money they had earned to the featured charity so we could assess if the video influenced behavior.

It will not surprise you at this stage of the book to know that people spent longer watching videos that were more immersive. All the immersive videos had well-structured narratives that gave people a reason to keep watching. Charitable appeals that jumped from scene to scene without a storyline were quickly skipped. Here is the most interesting finding: the longer people watched, the more money they donated to charity even though they were under no obligation to do so. One-quarter of the videos were so immersive that participants watched them in their entirety, and these charities received the most donations. Participants stopped watching videos when they were neurologically frustrated. That is, videos were stopped when people were paying attention but the narrative did not induce emotional resonance. The study was ethical because participants were not deceived about the impact of their decisions in the study and could say no without any penalty. Freedom to say no also means freedom to say yes.

An ethical concern arises when influence is hidden. For example, most US college campuses have reduced the size of plates at dining halls to combat the "freshman 15" in which students gain weight when they have access to unlimited food. This approach has been called libertarian paternalism and "nudging" by Nobel laureate in economic sciences Richard Thaler and his collaborator, law professor Cass Sunstein. They argue that influencing choices in this way is libertarian because people can make whatever decisions they want, but it is paternalistic because choice architecture guides them toward "better" decisions. Nudges hide the lever of influence so that people are unaware of how their choices are being manipulated.

Another concern is unintended consequences. Well-intentioned nudges can result in unforeseen outcomes, even if they are rare. Removing doughnuts from the dining options may be a good idea. But what about the diabetic who has taken insulin and needs a doughnut to stabilize his blood sugar? He cannot choose whether or not to have a doughnut and is worse off. Mill's harm principle and libertarian paternalism are based on the assumption that there is little variation around the average so that only a small number of people are worse off. These approaches also presume that people can expend the cognitive effort to evaluate options when the influences on choices are hidden. Both assumptions run counter to neuroscientific findings.

The ability to say no to subtleties in choice architecture gets even more concerning since many nudges exploit cognitive biases. A nudge might cause someone to sign up for a credit card with a low introductory rate that later skyrockets. Another nudge is a "recommendation" to purchase an item. Recommendations are useful because they reduce cognitive load but also diminish the desire to comparison shop, which might uncover a better deal. Nudging that exploits cognitive biases strays into the unethical if the person is unaware he or she is being nudged. People value the autonomy to make their own life choices. Best practice is to make the sources of influence transparent and to make it easy for people to opt out.

The TARES test is a way to assess if a persuasive communication is ethical. This acronym stands for truthfulness, authenticity, respect, equity, and (social) responsibility. When communications meet the TARES criteria, they are honest, fair, and offer true benefits to the receiver. TARES can be used as a screen to determine if the influence of a message, experience, or training is ethical or not.

As social creatures, we are constantly trying to persuade those around us. But as long as there is no undue influence or coercion, the method of persuasion is known, and the target of persuasion can say no, it is ethical to persuade others.

## PSYCHOLOGICAL SAFETY AND PERSUASION

Psychological safety was described in Chapter 4 as neural bandwidth that enables new information to enter the brain. When psychological safety is low, people become risk-averse and focus on current costs, not future benefits. Without psychological safety, there is scant opportunity to persuade.

The first step in building psychological safety is ensuring that one is perceived as trustworthy. A warm introduction from someone you both know works best. Without an introduction, find a shared educational experience, a company, or a location where one has lived. I am obsessed with language and will make connections by guessing where someone's accent is from. "Virginia? I lived in Arlington in the late 1990s and loved it there" is often all it takes to demonstrate a shared experience. People are more likely to feel psychologically safe and therefore be persuaded by those who are similar to themselves.

In general, women inspire psychological safety more effectively than men, giving them a persuasion advantage. Sales data bear this out. A 2019 study reported that 86% of women met their sales quotas, while only 78% of men were able to. The analysis showed that high-performing women in sales emphasized connecting and collaborating, while men focused on achieving goals. Connection is the foundation of psychological safety, and we only connect to people who appear trustworthy. Women also have an empathy advantage, so they are perceived as helpful. This is the reason why the two most popular virtual assistants, Siri and Alexa, have female voices as the default. The female superpower of empathy means they more easily induce oxytocin release in others, influencing everything from political views to purchase decisions.

Humans are also physiologic mimics. As we discussed in Chapter 5, when we share others' emotional states, neural activity synchronizes. This happens not only for Immersion, but also for psychological safety. If a salesperson is relaxed, then he or she transmits psychological safety to a prospect. Physiologic transmission happens fluidly when the persuader and the target of persuasion have similar personality traits. Even when this is not the case, it is not difficult, with a bit of practice, to identify someone's personality type and communicate using their preferred type of language. While the so-called Big Five traits with the acronym OCEAN (openness, conscientiousness, extraversion, agreeableness, neuroticism) are the most statistically valid, I find the simplicity of the four-dimensional Myers-Briggs Type Indicator handy to use when I want to connect to others. Personality is revealed by the way people speak, the books they read, and the types of jobs they have. Either the Big Five or Myers-Briggs typology can help you communicate using the language of the person you want to persuade, increasing psychological safety and thereby influence.

One online study of 3.5 million people reported that persuasive messages designed to appeal to a target's dominant personality trait generated 40% more clicks and up to 50% more purchases compared to generic messages and those structured for nondominant personality traits. As an example, those whose dominant trait is agreeableness (Big Five) or equivalently feeling (Myers-Briggs) are persuaded when a course of action will help others. Technology now enables personality matching in real time. Many large call centers use speech analytics software to match a caller's personality to that of a customer service agent by analyzing a few snippets of speech. When callers and service agents have similar personalities, problems are more likely to be resolved and to be handled more rapidly. This is the "people like us" approach on steroids.

## THE PERSUASION EQUATION

In addition to measuring Immersion during the 2016 Republican debates, we also measured Immersion while Democratic candidates for president debated. Since most swing voters are weakly affiliated Democrats, it is surprising that former US Secretary of State Hillary Clinton did not persuade enough of these folks to vote for her. Mrs. Clinton and Vermont Senator Bernie Sanders faced each other as the two Democratic primary candidates on March 9, 2016. Similar to the previous study, we measured Immersion while Democrats who were planning to vote in the California primary watched the debate live in my lab.

At the time, polls showed that voters favored Mrs. Clinton by a huge margin, and she was allowed to speak 31% longer during the debate than did Mr. Sanders. Yet, averaging across the one-hour event, Immersion was 11% higher in Democratic voters when Mr. Sanders spoke compared to Immersion for Mrs. Clinton. As with any long event, the brain continually returns to baseline so differences in Immersion tend to be small. To dig in deeper, we analyzed Immersion during the two-minute closing statements that viewers tend to focus on. During this period, Immersion for Mr. Sanders averaged fifty-four out of one hundred while Mrs. Clinton only produced Immersion in Democratic voters of five out of one hundred. Put another way, Mr. Sanders produced ten times more Immersion in Democratic voters during the closing statements than Mrs. Clinton did. While her performance in this debate was dreadful, Mrs. Clinton was nevertheless chosen to be the Democratic nominee for president. I have no doubt that Mrs. Clinton was qualified to be US president, but our data showed that her robotic communication did not produce enough of an emotional response to motivate people to get off their couches and vote. Post-election analysis by the Pew Research Center showed that among swing voters, 48% voted for Trump while 42% voted for Clinton. This changed the election outcome.

Persuasion requires sufficient Immersion in a message to provoke action. Contextual relevance directly impacts how much energy the brain devotes to information. We discussed this in Chapter 2 regarding smokers who saw pictures of cigarette packages. Storytelling is the most effective way to establish relevance and immerse the brain. Start a persuasive message with a hot open to capture dopaminergic attention, but not so aggressively that it degrades psychological safety, causing the message to fall on deaf neural ears. For this reason, fear appeals should be used with great care. An effective persuader will ask the target of persuasion to take an action during a peak Immersion moment.

Knitting together the principles we have discussed throughout the book leads to a formula you can use to be certain you can persuade. It has the acronym SIRTA—Staging, Immersion, Relevance, Target, and Action—that you can remember as "SIRTAin" (certain). These factors orient the brain's cost-benefit calculation toward benefits, increasing the likelihood of persuasion. Each of the SIRTA steps is necessary to influence behavior. If one step is missing, then the ability to influence others will flounder. Let's discuss each in turn.

**Staging** establishes psychological safety prior to the message as the precondition for influence. As we discussed previously, psychological safety creates the neural bandwidth so that the persuasion target can absorb information. When people are anxious, stressed, harried, distracted, or angry, they lack the neural resources to grasp information unless it immediately solves their crisis. One way for a persuader to create psychological safety is by using social proof, showing that "people like us" are doing the desired action. Staging also dictates the timing and placement of a message. Immediately after Walter Cronkite interrupted daytime programming to announce that President John F. Kennedy had been shot, an upbeat commercial for Nescafé instant coffee was shown as scheduled. The shock viewers felt over Kennedy's assassination inhibited their ability to absorb the message claiming that instant coffee would improve their lives. What precedes a message is as important as the message itself. Try this in your next in-person meeting: ask everyone to silence their phones. This not only removes distractions, but it primes those in the room to follow your directions, making the next thing you ask them to do easier.

**Immersion** crafts a message so that people's brains identify it as valuable. Immersion moves the brain out of homeostasis so that the cognitive and emotional content in the message are recognized. As we discussed in Chapter 2, immersive messages typically have a narrative structure and have product-story congruence in which the promoted action resolves the crisis the characters face. Immersion taps into the "monkey see, monkey do" hypersociality of the human brain.

**Relevance** determines the amount of neural processing devoted to a message. As we discussed in Chapter 2, the term of art for this in neuroscience is *top-down control*. The top part (cortex) of the brain ramps up activation in regions that process information when the information is relevant to a person's needs. Relevance supercharges the effect of an immersive message. Conversely, top-down control reduces neural activity when information is irrelevant. For example, your brain will enjoy a compelling commercial for Huggies diapers, but if you do not have an infant or toddler at home, your brain will rapidly discard the information. If you do have a baby (and she is not wailing so powerfully that Staging is inhibited), a message with high Immersion is highly valued. Relevant messages are easily recalled by cues such as visuals, logos, or music from the message; cued recall increases the likelihood of influence.

**Target** identifies people who will love a message. The likelihood of persuasion is increased by identifying superfans who are deeply immersed in the message. Superfans not only act after a message; they will share the information with others, leveraging message influence. To activate superfans, messages need to be customized to fit demographic and psychographic profiles by using locations, language, music, and other iconography that draw on memories of similar experiences. Finding superfans also reveals how to narrowcast messages. Companies know their target demographic from sales data. But they must establish if a particular message will immerse that demographic or a different one. Sometimes it is more cost effective to release existing content that effectively targets a non-core demographic rather than creating new content for a brand's core constituency. Measurement of Immersion often identifies unexpected pockets of superfans.

**Action** after a message is more likely when the need is urgent. Immersion is like tension in the brain as we saw in Chapter 1. A target of persuasion dissipates the tension of a message by taking an action. As a result, a call to action at an Immersion peak will be the most effective. Traditionally, calls to action are done at the end of a message when the narrative resolves and Immersion has declined. Content creators should edit messages so that Immersion peaks during the call to action at the end, or they should place the call to action in the middle of a message when Immersion is highest. The friction of taking an action should be reduced so that people act when tension is high. Most TV commercials are posted to YouTube but are not edited with a hyperlink to buy. Now. Now is the time; make it easy. Always remember that emotions are what move markets.

The formula is Persuasion = Staging + Immersion + Relevance + Target + Action.

Preferences are malleable to an extent. When information is relevant, immersive, and repeated, the brain will potentiate pathways that modify default neural and behavioral responses.

The brain is a learning organ and even old dogs can learn new tricks if the tricks are presented properly.

Learning new tricks can be enjoyable. In the final chapter, we will see how immersive experiences can improve people's quality of life.

## KEY TAKEAWAYS

1. To persuade, first create psychological safety.
2. Then connect to others with empathy.
3. Persuasion is more effective when the message is repeated to firmly establish it in memory.
4. The message should be tailored to the listener's personality type.
5. To provoke action, tell an immersive story that builds tension that can be released with a decision.

# CHAPTER 8

# THE BUSINESS OF HAPPINESS

British poet Alfred, Lord Tennyson, wrote in 1850 that "Nature [is] red in tooth and claw." Without a doubt, biology is cruel. And unfair. And cares not a whit about you and me. Unless of course you are able to get your precious genes into future generations. Then you are a winner.

The predominant doctrine in biology is that you are simply a gene replication machine. If biology dictates that only the strongest survive, why do people perform acts of kindness toward others? And why, pray tell, are humans obsessed with being happy? Monthly surveys report happiness trends and governments have spawned agencies to measure gross national happiness. Yet the biological imperative is to survive and sustain your gene line.

Recent research from my lab and others has shown that the

sources of happiness can be found in the brain and profoundly affect the quality of people's lives. There is good and bad news from this research. About one-half of life satisfaction is due to the genes your parents gifted to you. There is little you can do to affect this. But you can influence the other 50% through the choices you make and the experiences in which you choose to participate.

This chapter will explain why extraordinary experiences add to the quality of life and how you can make choices that will systematically increase the satisfaction you get from life. You are more than a gene replication machine, and there are good reasons why people are obsessed with happiness.

## EVOLUTION

All species struggle to survive and strive to reproduce. A chance mutation about 200,000 years ago made early *Homo sapiens* more sensitive to social information. This mutation increased the number of oxytocin receptors in the brain's frontal lobe, enabling our ancestors to not only understand what others were doing cognitively, but also experience the emotions of others. This helped early humans survive by enabling them to draw on social resources more effectively.

Over time, the mutation spread. Rather than being limited to living in small bands of kin-based groups as our genus had for millions of years, *Homo sapiens* could live in increasingly larger and more complex societies because they could intuit others' intentions. The most basic social information is the intention to help or harm. As culture flourished, societies developed norms in which helpers were embraced and the selfish and violent were ostracized. Since humans have long memories, being accepted back into a community after a serious norm violation was unlikely. As a result, being shunned by one's group was often a death sentence.

We became truly social creatures when the brain network that oxytocin activates allowed us to determine who to trust. Knowing when to trust strangers led to large-scale societies. In these communities, an individual's survival depended on many others. Cooperation among nonkin provided social insurance against a bad crop or an unsuccessful hunt. Communities began to function like superorganisms in which each segment nourished the other parts.

When I was doing field research in the rainforest of Papua New Guinea, I was embedded in a small tribe of subsistence farmers. Every family in the tribe tended a plot of land to grow food. There was no reason to put in extra work to grow a surplus because markets were far away and there was no electricity for refrigeration, so food spoiled quickly. Some dry goods, such as woven baskets, were sold in markets that tribe members could walk to in two or three days, but the trouble of doing this was barely balanced by the meager return. Food sharing was common in the tribe, but social insurance in the rainforest ended at the village boundary due to communication barriers and fear of outsiders; there are more than 800 distinct languages in Papua New Guinea and violent intertribal clashes are common. This lifestyle is similar to how our ancestors lived before civilizations arose 10,000 years ago.

Civilizations conglomerate thousands and sometimes millions of people. This enabled labor specialization, which drove widely distributed social insurance. One city's output could be traded for another's in the social superorganism. Trade among strangers reinforced the social norms of cooperation and trustworthiness as well as swift punishment for violators. Some scholars have argued that *Homo sapiens* should be renamed *Homo reciprocans* because of our propensity to cooperate with each other. Indeed, studies show that our brains guide us to reciprocate with strangers as a default response.

Norms of cooperation evolved into what it means to be a "good" or "virtuous" person. Virtue is valued by others beyond trade because it makes quotidian encounters safer and more pleasant. Our social nature evolved into a preference to be around virtuous people.

The oxytocin-enhanced ability to share others' emotions means that, in most cases, those who smile and appear friendly are safe to be around. Happiness became a signal of virtue. Not a perfect signal (think of con men), but a reasonably good signal. Virtuous people are happy in part because they have strong social networks that provide reciprocal emotional support. That is how happiness became important for human beings.

## HAPPINESS VS. FLOURISHING

One can try to fake being happy, but humans leak out "tells" that reveal our true emotional states, just like people's brains could identify CEOs who were making insincere apologies. For example, genuinely happy smiles, known as Duchenne smiles, crinkle the skin at the corners of one's eyes. Even if you did not know this explicitly, intuitively you can recognize when people are truly happy or just faking it. Think of how a child told to smile at a photography studio looks when bearing their teeth, and you have seen a non-Duchenne smile. Although many a rock star has tried, unbridled hedonism does not lead to a fulfilled life. Excessive sex, gambling, drugs, and alcohol may make people temporarily euphoric, but over time these pleasures lose their kick, negatively impact physical and emotional health, and undermine relationships. The ability to flourish throughout one's lifetime was called *eudaimonia* by the ancient Greeks and translates into flourishing or satisfaction with life.

Here's the key insight from neuroscience that brings us back to business practice: extraordinary experiences increase one's long-term satisfaction with life. The neurochemicals of Immersion provide a small jolt of joy that adds to our sense of flourishing and counteract negative emotions. Our brains crave immersive experiences not only because they are acutely enjoyable, but because they add to our long-term quality of life. They do this by strengthening pathways in the brain that prepare people to have extraordinary experiences in the future. By strengthening the "wiring" of brain networks for eudaimonia, the brain is ready to be immersed in an awe-inspiring experience. These could be as humble as meeting your smiling neighbor or as profound as watching a sunrise at Machu Picchu.

Let's return to Tennyson. The line before "tooth and claw" reads, "And love Creation's final law." When customer experiences are provided with love, customers will crave more of them. The same is true for advertising, movies, and corporate presentations. When these give customers joy, they tap into deep evolutionary desires for connection with others. All business is ultimately personal because humans are social creatures.

## SOCIAL PURPOSE

Doug Rauch was the president of quirky private label California grocer Trader Joe's in the 1990s when they were considering expanding nationally. Rauch told me that to do this successfully, he had to figure out the company's core purpose. After talking to customers and employees, Rauch had an epiphany: shopping at Trader Joe's was an opportunity to bring joy to people. They happened to do this by selling food to their customers, but the company's mission was clear: their employees had to create happiness.

Shopping at chain grocery stores is a chore, but Rauch thought that happiness was scalable and could be Trader Joe's unique offering. He modified every aspect of shopping at Trader Joe's so that it would be enjoyable. If you have shopped there, then you know that customers love the smiling faces, great service, and unusual selection. The chain quintupled its locations between 1990 and 2001 and increased its profits tenfold, generating more revenue per square foot than any other US grocer. Trader Joe's now has more than 500 stores and consistently ranks number one in customer satisfaction compared to its peers.

The traditional view is that businesses exist to solve customers' problems. The modern approach is that businesses that want long-term success need to bring joy to customers. Joy is the foundation for the experience economy. Neurologic Immersion correlates with enjoyment and builds a desire to repeat the experience. This is both a scientific reason to create the extraordinary for customers and also a moral argument. Amazing customer experiences improve customers' emotional and physical health and might even extend their lives. At the same time, businesses that offer extraordinary experiences to their customers will consistently grow profits because customers' brains want to re-experience the extraordinary.

## THE DEMAND FOR EXTRAORDINARY EXPERIENCES

While everyone's brain values extraordinary experiences, experiments from my lab show that some people value them more than others. Those who yearn for immersive experiences are relatively underserved and constitute a profitable demographic. One group, as we discussed in Chapter 2, are those with high affect intensity. These folks live in the sensation space and actively seek out immersive experiences. They enjoy social activities and especially value ones that are novel and intense. Examples are rock climbing, skydiving, and riding the longest zip line in North America that I rode with my daughter at the San Diego Zoo Safari Park, which took us over an enclosure of lions. These experiences will be more valued when they are done with another person. Think tandem zip lines rather than singletons. Building "social" into an experience nearly always increases its Immersion.

Intense experiences do not have to be life-threating. Hidden Worlds Entertainment has created an immersive aquatic experience in which guests are guided on ocean quests led by actors portraying famous explorers like Amelia Earhart.*

---

\* I am an unpaid advisor to Hidden Worlds Entertainment.

These quests are complemented by an exotic dining experience with dishes presented in unconventional ways. A portion of the profits support ocean health initiatives, and patrons are engaged by the company weeks before they attend and weeks afterward, creating an enjoyable ocean experience with social impact. Hidden Worlds Entertainment has packed each part of the customer experience with social interactions that they have designed and refined to be highly immersive.

The second demographic that yearns for immersive experiences may surprise you: senior citizens. Research from my lab, funded by the National Institute on Aging, has shown that the production of oxytocin from a social experience increases linearly with age. After retirement, people's social interactions are reduced and continue to fall as they age. This creates pent-up demand for socially-immersive experiences.

Neurologic Immersion by seniors has a strong positive correlation with life satisfaction in an unusual way. My research showed that the most immersed seniors in a social experience donated more money to charity and spent more time volunteering. Their brains were primed to connect to and help others. They also had more empathy for those around them and expressed more gratitude for their lives. Their satisfaction with life came from their service to others. These results continue to hold if religious activities are removed statistically, as older people tend to be more religious than younger people. Data from my lab and others show that immersive experiences extend health spans and life spans. Creating immersive experiences for seniors not only serves an underserved population; it also demonstrably improves their lives.

This research was the foundation for a new product developed by a company that manages active-living facilities. The company gifted Apple Watches to residents and obtained their permission to track their neurologic states during waking hours. Activities, mood, energy, and health were all assessed. Psychological safety and Immersion together predicted residents' moods with 82% accuracy and predicted how much energy they had each day with 88% accuracy. Peak Immersion moments occurred when participants engaged in activities with other people, including socializing, participating in entertainment, and getting together at mealtimes. Senior citizens are a population that has both the demand for immersive activities and the resources to pay for them.

A third demographic that seeks extraordinary experiences are single adults and those who struggle with loneliness, whether they are in a relationship or not. The brain prods us to make social connections by activating its pain matrix when we are lonely. Short periods of loneliness are not very painful, but chronic loneliness is. Interacting with others reduces this pain. As discussed above, immersive experiences, especially moments of peak Immersion, train the brain to connect more easily to others. This sets the neural stage to reduce or eliminate loneliness by making it less difficult and more rewarding to form relationships. For example, the data show that divorced men display a greater desire for immersive social experiences than single or married males and typically more than females, though there is broad variation in the population.

## IMMERSION SUPERSTARS

One way to understand the impact of immersive experiences on the quality of life is to examine people of all ages who are in the highest quartile of Immersion. These Immersion virtuosos are substantially more satisfied with their lives, primarily because they have better relationships. Those with romantic partners have more sex and rate their relationship quality as excellent. Immersion stars also have closer relationships with family and friends, including high levels of social support and greater resilience to setbacks. They even report that they are friends with themselves. In experiments in which participants could anonymously send money to others, those with high Immersion were more generous toward strangers even though they had no obligation to share with them. They also did not drink excessively and had few indicators of depression. Age, gender, weight, and sexual orientation did not affect these findings.

The relationship between Immersion and life satisfaction is most likely bidirectional: the brains of people who have great relationships have adapted to release more oxytocin which, in turn, improves their Immersion in experiences and in people. The brain tunes itself by building a model of what it expects to happen. Strong social connections prepare the brain to have extraordinary experiences, strengthening the neural networks that support Immersion in movies, advertisements, and shopping.

There are a number of ways that those who are lonely can build up their Immersion muscles and make connecting to others easier. The simplest way is to adopt a dog as we discussed in Chapter 6. Dogs were created by humans to manifest our best qualities. People with dogs are considered more trustworthy compared to the dogless. When I am hiking alone, women seldom approach me since safety is paramount. But when I have my German shepherd Buddy with me, men, women, and children will cross the trail to say hello and give Buddy a stroke. Walking a dog is a great way to meet one's neighbors, make friends, and talk to potential romantic partners. In the dog study discussed in Chapter 6, people who played with dogs shared 25% more money with strangers when given the chance compared to those in the cat group. This experimental finding indicates that the oxytocin burst dogs give us carries over to connecting to others more easily outside the lab.

These data suggest that dogs might train us to form immersive relationships. The brain's Immersion architecture is adaptive and helps us connect to pets and people without discriminating between them. As a result, dogs can jump-start the Immersion to quality of life feedback loop. Other research from my lab has shown that dogs love their owners more than cats do. That is, after playing with their humans, dogs release 400% more oxytocin than do cats. Businesses that are dog-friendly have a natural Immersion advantage. British pubs know this, and many US microbreweries similarly open their doors to patrons with pooches. Starbucks will make a whipped-cream-topped "puppuccino" for patrons with dogs, and retailers from Apple stores, to Home Depot, to Bass Pro Shops encourage customers to bring their dogs along while they shop.

Another hack to train the brain for Immersion is the use of social media. Research from my lab has demonstrated that the brain processes connections on social media the same way as in-person interactions but with 25–50% less Immersion. While too much social media use can crowd out real-life relationships, neurologically, any connection is better than no connection. Businesses can supercharge product use by facilitating social connections among users. Fitness tracking platform Strava encourages users to share their workouts on social media and makes connections to nearby athletes so people can train together. Strava also solicits suggestions to improve their product on social media, showing through transparency that they are partners with users. Exercise equipment maker Peloton, too, has added a social layer to its workouts and is evolving into a social media company. A growing portion of toymaker Mattel's products are internet-connected, enabling what the company calls "mixed play" with kid-safe social connections.

Affective robots are another technological approach to stimulate Immersion. These devices simulate emotional responses and offer isolated people the benefit of quasi-social connections. For example, a baby harp seal robot called Paro responds to touch and verbal commands, makes eye contact, and moves its tail when stroked. Data show that isolated individuals, especially older people, rapidly form attachments to Paro, with some saying that they cannot imagine life without it.

Another hack to kick-start the Immersion network in the brain is to form connections at one's place of work. As we discussed in Chapter 6, the office should be a social-emotional hub. This will motivate employees who have the freedom to work remotely to come into the office. Even for hybrid employees, adding a Slack channel to post personal news and random thoughts is an effective way to add a social layer. Motivate the social aspects of work by organizing a Friday happy hour, or a pizza lunch, or a weekend activity to connect to work colleagues. Smart leaders are likely to cover the costs of these events in order to facilitate social connections and improve teamwork. I worked for a boss who brought in doughnuts on Fridays. I'm not a junk food eater, but I and everyone else appreciated the gesture. I may have even gobbled a doughnut a few times. As we will see, gift-giving is a key way to sustain relationships.

## THE GIFT IS NOT ABOUT THE GIFT

Aarhus University in Denmark has one of the premier brain-imaging centers in the world. I go to Aarhus every year to work with collaborators and enjoy living for a month or two in Denmark's second city. In the winter, Denmark is a land of cold and darkness and struggle. Danes embrace their Viking roots by bundling up their babies in the winter and putting them in strollers outdoors while they shop or dine. This hardens children to the Arctic cold. Many Danes are also hardened emotionally—they can be wonderfully warm yet don't feel a constant need to show emotions. The suppressed emotions of Danes offered a chance to test whether Immersion flows between couples when giving a gift. A 130-year-old chocolate company agreed to fund such a study.

A tradition at Anthon Berg explains why they would fund my research. Just before Christmas a few years after Mr. Berg opened his tiny confectionary shop in 1884, customers were queued up in the howling Copenhagen wind. Mr. Berg saw how dedicated his customers were and joined them outside, giving each a marzipan-filled chocolate treat. The company memorialized his benevolence with the slogan "You can never be too generous."

I, too, am known for generosity. In 2010, *Fast Company* magazine gave me the nickname "Dr. Love" for my research showing that oxytocin is the neurochemical source of generosity and love. The quid pro quo for the funding was that Anthon Berg would turn my experiment into a promotional film. They were betting that the film might solve a problem they faced. Danish men did not buy their partners chocolates for Valentine's day, believing that it was just an "American holiday." Could the science of Immersion convince men that it was in their best interest to give gifts of chocolate in February?

The agency enlisted Niels Nørløv Hansen, a well-known Danish filmmaker, to direct the film. A lab was built for me in a Copenhagen TV studio so Hansen could film the entire experiment using nine cameras behind two-way mirrors. The producers recruited thirty-two heterosexual Danish couples to participate in the study. Some couples had been together for six months and others for sixty years. The men were instructed to write down why their partner was special and to read this while they gave her a box of Anthon Berg chocolates. My job was to measure neurologic responses during the gift presentation. Since Danes suppress their emotions so much, I doubted that the older men had told their wives that they loved them since the day they were married. The suppressed emotions of Danes biased the experiment against finding Immersion contagion during gift-giving. But if we found that Immersion reflected from women back to men in Denmark, it is likely that this response happens everywhere.

The data showed that average oxytocin increased 27.5% in men immediately after gift-giving, a statistically significant increase from baseline. We also measured men's change in happiness, and it shot up too. The data showed that a gift is not just about stuff. Gifts physiologically connect us to others.

In 2021, businesses in the US spent $242 billion on gifts. Companies understand that gifts create a neural desire to reciprocate. Gifts are effective marketing tools, but one should ensure that the size of the gift is commensurate with the size of the relationship. Customers who make annual purchases that rank in the top 5% should garner larger gifts than an entry-level customer who might get a token gift. Rather than sending a generic Christmas present, use data from customer relationship management software to give a present on the anniversary of the client's first purchase. Or present a gift a week after their next major purchase. This establishes a relationship between the behavior (the purchase) and the gift in the brain. Present the gift in person at the client's office so colleagues can see how special they are, increasing the impact of gift-giving. Over 80% of companies report that gifts have improved relationships with customers, and 48% believe that gifts have substantially improved customer loyalty. Anthon Berg was right—generosity is good business.

## RITUALS

In addition to gifts, rituals like Valentine's Day generate a wave of Immersion. These are enhanced neurologically if, as the Danes discovered, one uses the ritual to share feelings. The first field study I ever did measured oxytocin at a wedding by taking blood samples. Sure enough, weddings are immersive, most powerfully for the bride, the groom, and their parents. The evolutionary purpose of weddings is to ensure couples successfully replenish the pool of humans. This is more likely when there are strong emotional bonds between partners as well as with their family and friends. The wedding ritual delivers this.

This study and related studies from my lab show that rituals are neurologically valued. Conventional wisdom is that people tire of repeating the same experience. But research shows that rituals increase psychological safety, providing the foundation for an immersive and enjoyable experience. I ran an experiment for NHK TV in Japan that used before and after blood draws during a twenty-minute unpartnered New England folk dance. The data showed that the neurochemical pillars of Immersion surged when people danced. The attentional response (ACTH) went up by 16% and oxytocin increased by 11%. Immersion also increased dancers' connection to members of their group by 21% and to "something bigger than oneself" by 69%. Rituals are powerful ways to forge connections.

This experiment and others measuring brain responses prove that the most effective way to increase Immersion is through coordinated movement. This is why romantic partners are wooed by dancing. It is easier to move in synchrony when there is a beat: soldiers learn to march in bootcamp by calling out cadences. Coordinated movement produces Immersion for strangers as well as for friends and lovers.

Movement can be as subtle as signs on the floor showing patrons how to move through IKEA stores. Building movement into consumer experiences, both in-person and online, will similarly increase Immersion. For example, pairing up customers who are looking for similar items can generate Immersion, as can using artificially intelligent apps to guide groups of shoppers in an online or physical store as if they are on a quest together. Shopping experiences can be gamified to capture the immersive effects of coordination. Imagine being "knighted" if you are on a social shopping quest and you find the product group members want first. Customers can be crowned "kings" or "queens" if they check out with the most valuable basket of items during each quest. Gamified marketing can generate coordinated movements as people search for hidden "Easter eggs" in commercials or find "gold" in augmented reality. As with gift giving, brands that induce coordination benefit from the transference of Immersion from the experience to the product.

## SATISFIED EMPLOYEES

Rituals can be used to motivate employees by creating opportunities to connect, just like Zappos's sumo wrestling experience. Danish pump manufacturer Grundfos holds an annual "Olympics" in which over 1,000 colleagues from multiple nations compete in various sports and bond with each other. Other rituals are customer-focused. We discussed the selling ceremony in Chapter 5, and this can be ritualized by including sights, sounds, and smells. Managers at Trader Joe's ring a brass ship's bell when more cashiers are needed, providing an aural ritual for employees and shoppers. Trader Joe's employees are also known to break into song to soothe crying toddlers.

Businesses that observe rituals create value beyond the products and services they sell. As we discussed in Chapter 6, if employees are immersed in what they are doing, this will "infect" customers with Immersion. Customer-facing employees must want to create happiness, whether they are selling insurance, cars, or candy. Hiring employees who have the personality traits of agreeableness and empathy is the first step in creating a happiness-inducing service experience, as these folks are more immersed in every social experience. In addition, studies in positive psychology show that those with the character strengths of humor and zest—the latter describing those who have a sense of excitement and energy—enjoy their jobs more. When these traits are combined with a transcendent purpose, that is, how the organization's work benefits society, employees have a calling, not just a job. Customer service rituals done by employees need to be rehearsed so they are fluid and enjoyable, even with cranky clients.

The Danish are among the happiest people on the planet for a number of reasons, with an important one being their culture of "hygge." The word *hygge* means "to give courage, comfort, and joy" and is a treasured part of their cultural identity. The Danes practice hygge by creating a cozy atmosphere where people can hang out and connect with each other over food and drinks, often surrounded by nature. Bringing the warmth and care of hygge into your business is good business. Large windows, indoor plants, comfortable couches, and welcoming employees are the ingredients that businesses can use to create hygge. ESRI, the first and largest geographic information system software company, built a plant-filled solarium at their Redlands, California, headquarters. Employees use the space to eat and, with Wi-Fi throughout, to work with hygge.

The psychological safety and trust hygge liberates in employees carries over to interactions with customers. Taking the time to practice hygge daily is an investment in both employee retention and customer loyalty. When care and comfort are foremost, price is less important. Every product or service is bundled with an experience. Make the experience comfortable and immersive and customers will want to repeat it.

## THE BUSINESS OF LOVE

A growing number of businesses have moved beyond creating extraordinary experiences in advertising, entertainment, and customer service to engineering the most profound experience most of us will ever have: falling in love.

Years ago, I was interviewed by the women's magazine *Redbook* about the science of human connection. The journalist identified me as a "relationship expert," something I would never call myself, but the title stuck. I have served as a relationship expert on the *Dr. Phil* show, was asked to create a Valentine's Day experiment for NBC's *Today* show, and was invited to work with Ben Higgins on a soundstage in Los Angeles.

I told Ben to remove his shirt. I needed to attach electrocardiogram wires to his chest. Then I put sensors on his hand to measure his electrodermal arousal from the women he would soon meet. Brushing aside his hair, I fit an electroencephalograph to his head to measure his attentional responses.

Ben is twenty-six years old and is looking for love. Desperately looking for love.

Okay, shirt back on. No, wait. The cameras are rolling and the producer wants Ben shirtless.

Welcome to ABC's hit TV show *The Bachelor*.

After a string of failed relationships, Ben Higgins agreed to let TV producers help him find a wife. Ben had been a contestant on ABC's *The Bachelorette*, and now he was the headliner on *The Bachelor*'s 20th season. Episode 1 opened with Ben meeting twenty-seven women for the first time at a cocktail party. Every woman expressed her interest in marrying attractive and personable Ben.

By the end of the evening, Ben had eliminated seven of the women as potential spouses. How did Ben know who to send home? And how would Ben decide that a woman was "the one"?

Dr. John Gottman was one of the first clinician-scientists to use physiologic measures to understand relationships. Gottman and colleagues were able to predict with 80% accuracy which couples would divorce during a fourteen-year period by quantifying physiologic arousal and conversational style while they discussed a contentious topic. Gottman showed that newlyweds who had high arousal were more likely to divorce than those who maintained equanimity. I wanted to do the opposite on *The Bachelor*: predict which woman Ben would propose to by measuring neurologic Immersion the first time they went on a date (with cameras rolling, of course). Ben offered roses each week to the women who were still in competition for a marriage proposal.

While few people date on a TV show, the online dating market is large and growing. About one-third of Americans use a dating app, spending around six hours per week looking for love at an average cost of $132 per year. Online dating generated $3.6 billion in revenue in 2021 and is growing at 7% annually. Men use dating apps 70% more than women do and are twice as likely to pay for a date. The average American spends $700 per year to go on dates with romantic partners. At the same time, 750,000 married couples in the US divorce annually, spending an average of $13,000 in legal fees alone to untie the knot. Failed marriages are not only financially costly, but they radically reduce both partners' satisfaction with their lives. Before helping Ben find love, I wanted to test my approach at small scale and see if I could help a few couples improve their relationships.

## REPAIRING MARRIAGES

Crying was not what I expected. Natsumi might have been crying for joy. Or maybe relief. It was difficult to tell since the conversation was in Japanese. Her husband sat stone-faced, so I pushed him closer to her and told him to hug her. He did, gingerly.

Earlier that day, Natsumi had looked into a camera and said that she had been contemplating divorce from her husband, Keisuke, for the last two years. She and Keisuke were in their early thirties and had two little boys. The couple lived in the Tokyo suburbs, and while she worked close to home, he spent an hour and a half on the train going into the city and then another hour and a half coming home. Keisuke helped little around the house or with his kids, and when I was with them he showed Natsumi little affection.

A marriage is really on the rocks when the wife says to a

national audience that she wants a divorce. Japan's state-funded broadcaster, NHK, had asked me to design immersive experiences for a two-part special they were producing called *Japanese Marriage in Crisis*. The program examined the growing number of middle-aged Japanese women initiating divorce from their husbands. The reasons given for divorce confirmed Japanese stereotypes: the men worked too much and treated their wives like furniture. Many women said they could not bear staying married for another thirty or forty years, given the long Japanese life expectancy.

An NHK film crew, my colleague Jorge Barraza, and I spent a full day at Keisuke and Natsumi's house. First, Jorge and I measured Keisuke's and Natsumi's baseline Immersion in each other while they sat at their dinner table. I hoped that the activities I had designed would increase Immersion in each other and, in the best case, stave off divorce.

Keisuke and Natsumi were willing to give it a try but moved like robots, just going through the motions; there was no fun, no spark, no joy. An hour into the TV shoot, I feared that their marriage was beyond fixing. After I gave them some coaching, they finally loosened up and seemed to enjoy being together.

During the course of the day, both Natsumi's and Keisuke's Immersion in each other increased about 20% from baseline. Equally important, just like the couple shopping for their dream home, Natsumi's and Keisuke's Immersion synchrony also improved over time. They were connecting. Natsumi cried when she saw the data, saying, "I never knew my husband really cared about me." That is when I pushed stock-still Keisuke to hug his wife.

Even when it comes to love, data matter. Objective data can help couples identify what they can do to increase their Immersion in each other without having to intuit how the other person is feeling. As we discussed in Chapter 1, feelings are vague and fleeting when appraised consciously. Having a measure that removes the history of slights and fights can be a relief. As we discussed above, the quality of one's romantic relationships has a profound effect on one's satisfaction with life, so measurement is worthwhile. A number of companies now offer technologies to measure emotional states, but as of this writing, most are focused on stress reduction rather than on a partner's emotions. This is a large and underserved market opportunity.

Unfulfilling marriages motivate partners to spend time alone, reducing the quality of life. Swapping one hundred minutes a day of time spent alone for time with one's spouse increases life satisfaction for the average couple by 2.1 percentage points. Measurement of partners' Immersion can identify the most neurologically valuable way to spend this additional one hundred minutes. This could be as simple as a walk while holding hands or as bold as a zipline over a pride of lions.

Relationships have a profound effect on emotional and physical health. Americans between the ages of fifty and eighty who rated the quality of their romantic relationship in the top one-third have a 13% lower lifetime mortality risk compared to those who have lower-quality relationships. On the other end of the spectrum, if one's romantic partner is neurotic, relationship quality is typically low, as is life satisfaction. Even Benjamin Franklin recognized this, writing, "If these [neurotic] people will not change this bad habit...it is good for others to avoid an acquaintance with them, which is always disagreeable."

Given these substantial impacts, businesses that can improve relationships are thriving. Couples-only hotels, resorts, tours, and cruises have developed into a several-hundred-million-dollar business that helps couples connect. Wine tasting, experiential dining venues like Opaque Dining in the Dark or the Snow Castle restaurant made entirely of ice in Kemi, Finland, and gourmet cooking experiences are perfect for an immersive date night. Couples-focused day spas have similarly grown into a multibillion-dollar business. Physical activity done together, such as hiking, biking, or walking, is an easy way for couples to reconnect by synchronizing their Immersion. Activities give couples an opportunity to strengthen bodies as well as strengthen relationships.

## *THE BACHELOR* REDUX

Episode 2 of *The Bachelor* put Ben on a group date with seven of the remaining twenty ladies. The first impossible-not-to-watch experiment I designed for *The Bachelor* had Ben and one woman at a time sitting on a bed and caressing each other while my team measured Immersion. Ben wore white shorts and was shirtless, while the women had on white shorts and sports bras. The situation was so awkward for Ben and the women—caressing someone they had just met while a crew of twenty watched—that I had no idea if the data would show anything useful.

The producers included a pair of identical twins, Haley and Emily, among the seven women Ben would be caressing. This gave me a perfect "gut check" of data quality. If one twin's physiologic responses were not similar to the other twin's, I would doubt the validity of our measurements.

The data showed that the twins had almost identical Immersion in Ben (sixty-seven and sixty-eight out of one hundred). These values are quite high and indicated a strong attraction. This confirmed that the data were valid.

The other women's Immersion in Ben varied from twenty-four to seventy-five. The highest Immersion was from a contestant named Olivia. Olivia would become infamous in "Bachelor Nation" because she seemed vain and conniving and repeatedly expressed excitement by holding her mouth wide open.

We ran three other experiments, and in each one, Olivia was the most immersed in Ben. This is quite unusual. Beyond this, Ben's second-by-second Immersion in Olivia was among the highest values I have ever seen. They were almost perfectly in sync. Stacks of research have shown that synchrony predicts long-term happiness in relationships.

I shared the results with Ben on camera but told him not to put too much emphasis on the few experiments we had done; he could use or disregard our findings. At the end of the filming day, Ben gave Olivia a rose, keeping her from being dismissed. In fact, Olivia was the front-runner for a marriage proposal through week six. In week seven, she was ignominiously dumped by Ben and "left" on a deserted island. Ben eventually proposed to "Lauren B" who was not part of our experimental group.

Ben and Lauren B were together for two years but then ended

their engagement. Relationships that start on TV have a poor track record. Only two of the twenty-five seasons of *The Bachelor* have resulted in marriages, and of these, only one has lasted. Was Olivia the right woman for Ben? The data show that they were powerfully immersed in each other on the day we collected data. If their Immersion had continued to be that strong, they could very well have had a successful relationship.

Just like meeting someone at the right time in your life is important, so is having synchronous Immersion. Brain activity is not fixed but adapts to the environment you are in, including romantic environments. By choosing extraordinary experiences, especially those involving movement, like dancing or rock climbing or skiing, partners' brain activity will synchronize, building stronger emotional attachments.

## KEY TAKEAWAYS

1. Multiple demographics, including senior citizens and single adults, want immersive experiences but are underserved.
2. Adding a social layer to products and services increases Immersion and enjoyment.
3. Extraordinary experiences train the brain to connect to others and increase the quality of life.
4. Businesses that provide extraordinary experiences raise people's satisfaction with life and build loyal customer bases.
5. Love is an immersive experience, and businesses that serve customers with love are highly profitable.

# CONCLUSION

Immersion captures the social value of the interactions people have every day with family, friends, teachers, and at businesses. This book traced Immersion's development from laboratory science to use by the US military and intelligence community to a platform that nonscientists use every day to improve people's lives. Immersion is a prediction engine, accurately forecasting individual behaviors and market movements by convolving brain signals that process feelings. Immersion jolts the lazy brain out of idle mode and into relationship mode. Relationships are what people most value, and this is why immersive experiences inspire actions.

Each chapter shared actionable insights gleaned from measuring Immersion during experiences that varied from advertising to luxury retail to a fourth-grade classroom. As you get to work creating extraordinary experiences, it is worth reviewing the most effective ways to immerse participants.

It is easiest to produce Immersion for experiences that are

based on stories. Most prominent among these are advertising and entertainment. Yet without measuring Immersion, many advertisements fail to move markets, and the majority of TV shows and movies never find a broad audience. The good news is that content with average Immersion can generate a positive return on investment if enough superfans repeat the experience and spread their passion through social media; think of Liam, the Manchester United superfan who would do anything for his team and the cadre of young women who watched and rewatched *The Fault in Our Stars*. Superfans seek out content that is relevant to their lives and when they find it, their brains devote additional resources to the experience, driving up Immersion and enjoyment. Content can thrive in the long tail if a fan base can be identified and activated to support it.

In addition to building a narrative, the data show that content can be structured to intensify Immersion by, for example, building anticipation and breaking patterns. Using these techniques to create peaks in Immersion is especially important for experiences that last twenty minutes or longer, including movies and retail sales. In movies, multiple storylines that vary in tension let the brain recover so it can extract all the value from a peak moment. Immersion peaks are also accentuated by including multisensory elements such as music, scents, somatic sensations, and movement. Adding "social" to an experience supercharges Immersion—for example, the friendly cashier who reminds a loyalty program member that he or she has earned a free gift.

Immersion is, perhaps surprisingly, radically changing education and training by providing unbiased and predictive feedback to teachers and trainers. The growth of remote and asynchronous teaching demands that class time is active, social, and enjoyable. Online education providers like K12 and The Socratic Experience actively engage students in learning, enabling them to gain competency at their own rates using short, intensive expositions. Immersion predicts how much information learners absorb, enabling customization of coursework at scale. My research shows that high-Immersion classes effectively move information from short-term to long-term memory, the latter being the true measure of learning.

Immersion is also being built into retail shopping. Narrative retail is expanding from destinations like Bass Pro Shops and Apple stores to mid-market retailers. Walmart Neighborhood Markets are small-footprint grocery stores that combine low prices with friendly customer service. These stores, and similar retailers that elevate service, should focus on creating personal emotional connections, just like Zappos and Panera do. Great customer experiences are not only differentiators, but they drive up lifetime customer value. Indeed, my analysis shows that mid-priced retail outlets provide the most Immersion per dollar spent. But people should still occasionally splurge on the extraordinary in order to enjoy peak Immersion experiences.

To consistently provide extraordinary customer service, appropriate hiring and training are absolutely necessary. Then organizations must ensure that employees are psychologically safe so they have the neural bandwidth to create Immersion for customers and in their teams. Companies that have organized their offices as social-emotional hubs increase Immersion and the opportunities for unexpected "collisions" that generate new ideas. Immersion is more likely to occur when employees eat and drink together like the Swedes do with *fika*, when office design facilitates interactions, and when people bring dogs to work. Without Immersion, innovation withers and job satisfaction erodes. Autonomy also spurs innovation and is more likely for remote employees, but humans are social beings and perform best when they interact in person.

In addition to social interactions at work, aligning employees' strengths with tasks increases discretionary effort by building mastery. Mastery increases job satisfaction and provides the neural foundation for innovation. Neural job crafting efficiently identifies what employees' brains love doing by capturing Immersion peaks. Measuring Immersion at work often reveals hidden talents and opportunities for professional growth. Riding Immersion peaks makes a job feel less like work and more like a calling.

Immersion is a powerful tool, and it must be used with care. The SIRTA algorithm (Staging, Immersion, Relevance, Target, Action) is a neurologically informed way to persuade people to take an action. Communicating the benefits of actions that customers, audience members, and employees can take with high Immersion is ethical as long as people have the ability to say no. Indeed, when individuals benefit, immersive communications also support social goals such as protecting the environment or adopting new technologies. Immersive communications are the most effective way to motivate people to join together to improve the planet.

## WHY IMMERSION MATTERS

Just like the powerful emotional responses I had when I watched *La La Land*, immersive experiences add to the quality of life. This is why we seek them out, why our brains value them, and why we pay for them. Business is ultimately about serving others. The greatest service one can offer is an extraordinary experience, whether you are eating at Panera, shopping at Trader Joe's, or giving your partner Anthon Berg chocolates. Immersion signals that the extraordinary is happening, and when it does, businesses have the opportunity to completely satisfy a customer's needs. The extraordinary produces a desire to have the experience again, creating a loyal customer base. The neurochemical sources of Immersion are the same ones that are released when we fall in love. Providing the extraordinary to customers is an act of love.

# BIBLIOGRAPHY

## CHAPTER 1

Barraza, Jorge A., and Paul J. Zak. "Oxytocin Instantiates Empathy and Produces Prosocial Behaviors." In *Oxytocin, Vasopressin and Related Peptides in the Regulation of Behavior*, edited by Elena Choleris, Donald W. Pfaff, and Martin Kavaliers, 331–342. Cambridge: Cambridge University Press, 2013. https://doi.org/10.1017/CBO9781139017855.022.

Dutton, Donald G., and Arthur P. Aron. "Some Evidence for Heightened Sexual Attraction Under Conditions of High Anxiety." *Journal of Personality and Social Psychology* 30, no. 4 (1974): 510–517. https://doi.org/10.1037/h0037031.

Hurlemann, René, Alexandra Patin, Oezguer A. Onur, Michael X. Cohen, Tobias Baumgartner, Sarah Metzler, Isabel Dziobek, et al. "Oxytocin Enhances Amygdala-Dependent, Socially Reinforced Learning and Emotional Empathy in Humans." *Journal of Neuroscience* 30, no. 14 (2010): 4999–5007. https://doi.org/10.1523/JNEUROSCI.5538-09.2010.

Kosfeld, Michael, Markus Heinrichs, Paul J. Zak, Urs Fischbacher, and Ernst Fehr. "Oxytocin Increases Trust in Humans." *Nature* 435, no. 7042 (2005): 673–676. https://doi.org/10.1038/nature03701.

Lin, Pei-Ying, Naomi Sparks Grewal, Christophe Morin, Walter D. Johnson, and Paul J. Zak. "Oxytocin Increases the Influence of Public Service Advertisements." *PLoS ONE* 8, no. 2 (2013). https://doi.org/10.1371/journal.pone.0056934.

Smith, Jacquelyn. "The Worst Super Bowl Ads of All Time." *Forbes*, January 29, 2014. https://www.forbes.com/sites/jacquelynsmith/2014/01/29/the-worst-super-bowl-ads-of-all-time/?sh=5bf1223a2c76.

Willens, Michele. "FILM; Putting Films to the Test, Every Time." *New York Times*, June 26, 2020. https://www.nytimes.com/2000/06/25/movies/film-putting-films-to-the-test-every-time.html.

Zak, Paul J. *The Moral Molecule: The Source of Love and Prosperity*. New York: Dutton, 2012.

## CHAPTER 2

"Ghost Adventures: Sailors' Snug Harbor Pictures." Trvl Channel, accessed May 18, 2022. https://www.travelchannel.com/shows/ghost-adventures/photos/ghost-adventures-sailors-snug-harbor-pictures.

"Murder and Suicide on Staten Island; The Chaplain of the Sailor's Snug Harbor Shot and Instantly Killed by an Inmate of that Institution. Court of General Sessions. Before Judge McCunn." *New York Times*, February 1, 1863. https://www.nytimes.com/1863/02/01/archives/murder-and-suicide-on-staten-island-the-chaplain-of-the-sailors.html.

Barraza, Jorge A., Xinbo Hu, Elizabeth T. Terris, Chuan Wang, and Paul J. Zak. "Oxytocin Increases Perceived Competence and Social-Emotional Engagement with Brands." *PLoS ONE* 16, no. 11 (2021). https://doi.org/10.1371/journal.pone.0260589.

Barrett, Frederick S., and Petr Janata. "Neural Responses to Nostalgia-Evoking Music Modeled by Elements of Dynamic Musical Structure and Individual Differences in Affective Traits." *Neuropsychologia* 91 (2016): 234–246. https://doi.org/10.1016/j.neuropsychologia.2016.08.012.

Berns, Gregory S., and Sara E. Moore. "A Neural Predictor of Cultural Popularity." *Journal of Consumer Psychology* 22, no. 1 (2011): 154–160. https://doi.org/10.1016/j.jcps.2011.05.001.

Carr, Sam. "How Many Ads Do We See a Day in 2021?" PPC Protect, February 15, 2021. https://ppcprotect.com/blog/strategy/how-many-ads-do-we-see-a-day.

Cheung, Wing-Yee, Tim Wildschut, Constantine Sedikides, Erica G. Hepper, Jamie Arndt, and Ad J. J. M. Vingerhoets. "Back to the Future: Nostalgia Increases Optimism." *Personality and Social Psychology Bulletin* 39, no. 11 (2013): 1484–1496. https://doi.org/10.1177/0146167213499187.

Gray, Christopher. "Streetscapes/The Music Hall at Snug Harbor Cultural Center; A Low-Budget Revival for a Grand 1890 Theater." *New York Times*, April 7, 1996. https://www.nytimes.com/1996/04/07/realestate/streetscapes-music-hall-snug-harbor-cultural-center-low-budget-revival-for-grand.html.

Heaven, Douglas. "Why Faces Don't Always Tell the Truth about Feelings." *Nature*, February 26, 2020. https://www.nature.com/articles/d41586-020-00507-5.

Johnson, Lauren. "When Procter & Gamble Cut $200 Million in Digital Ad Spend, It Increased Its Reach 10%." Adweek, March 1, 2018. http://www.adweek.com/brand-marketing/when-procter-gamble-cut-200-million-in-digital-ad-spend-its-marketing-became-10-more-effective.

Leach, John. (2018). "'Give-up-itis' Revisited: Neuropathology of Extremis." *Medical Hypotheses* 120 (2018): 14–21. https://doi.org/10.1016/j/mehy.2018.08.009.

Lin, Pei-Ying, Naomi Sparks Grewal, Christophe Morin, Walter D. Johnson, and Paul J. Zak. "Oxytocin Increases the Influence of Public Service Advertisements." *PLoS ONE* 8, no. 2 (2013). https://doi.org/10.1371/journal.pone.0056934.

Nelson, Leif D., Tom Meyvis, and Jeff Galak. "Enhancing the Television-Viewing Experience Through Commercial Interruptions." *Journal of Consumer Research* 36, no. 2 (2009): 160–172. https://doi.org/10.1086/597030.

Nestor, Liam, Ella McCabe, Jennifer Jones, Luke Clancy, and Hugh Garavan. "Differences in 'Bottom-Up' and 'Top-Down' Neural Activity in Current and Former Cigarette Smokers: Evidence for Neural Substrates Which May Promote Nicotine Abstinence Through Increased Cognitive Control." *Neuroimage* 56, no. 4 (2011): 2258–2275. https://doi.org/10.1016/j.neuroimage.2011.03.054.

Spanier, Gideon. "P&G Slashes Ad Spend by $350M After Cutting 'Waste', Agency Fees." PR Week, August 8, 2019. https://www.prweek.com/article/1593429/p-g-slashes-ad-spend-350m-cutting-waste-agency-fees.

Wolff-Mann, Ethan. "Why Dos Equis' 'Most Interesting Man' Ad Campaign Was So Successful." *Time*, March 9, 2016. https://time.com/4252403/success-most-interesting-man-in-the-world-ad.

Wunsch, Nils-Gerrit. "Global Chocolate Consumption per Capita in 2017, by Country." Statista, May 17, 2021. https://www.statista.com/statistics/819288/worldwide-chocolate-consumption-by-country.

## CHAPTER 3

Askin, Noah, and Michael Mauskapf. "What Makes Popular Culture Popular? Product Features and Optimal Differentiation in Music." *American Sociological Review* 82, no. 5 (2017): 910–944. https://doi.org/10.1177/0003122417728662.

Craig, Shelley. "How Music Can Change a Film." April 13, 2012. Video, 3:26. https://www.youtube.com/watch?v=rn9V0cN4NWs&t=43s.

Filson, Darren, David Switzer, and Portia Besocke. "At the Movies: The Economics of Exhibition Contracts." *Economic Inquiry* 43, no. 2 (2007): 354–369. https://doi.org/10.1093/ei/cbi024.

Hooton, Christopher. "We Spoke to the People Who Make Film Trailers." *Independent online*, January 17, 2017. https://www.independent.co.uk/arts-entertainment/films/features/film-trailers-editors-interview-create-teasers-tv-spots-a7531076.html.

Houghton, Bruce. "24,000 Tracks Uploaded to Music Streamers Every 24 Hours." Hypebot, June 11, 2018. https://www.hypebot.com/hypebot/2018/06/24000-tracks-uploaded-to-music-streamers-every-24-hours.html.

Interiano, Myra, Kamyar Kazemi, Lijia Wang, Jienian Yang, Zhaoxia Yu, and Natalia L. Komorava. "Musical Trends and Predictability of Success in Contemporary Songs in and Out of the Top Charts." *Royal Society Open Science* 5, no. 171274 (2018). https://doi.org/10.1098/rsos.171274.

Lodderhose, Diana. "Sony's Pictures Division Reports Loss of $719M; Company's Overall Net Profit Takes 50% Hit." Deadline, April 27, 2017. http://deadline.com/2017/04/sony-pictures-division-reports-719-loss-overall-net-profit-down-half-1202078945.

McFee, Brian, Thierry Bertin-Mahieux, Daniel P. W. Ellis, and Gert R. G. Lanckriet. "The Million Song Dataset Challenge." *WWW '12 Companion: Proceedings of the 21st International Conference on World Wide Web* (2012): 909–916. https://doi.org/10.1145/2187980.2188222.

Navarro, José Gabriel. "Number of Cinema Screens Worldwide in 2021, by Region & Format." Statista, March 15, 2022. https://www.statista.com/statistics/255353/number-of-cinema-screens-worldwide-by-region-and-format/.

Setoodeh, Ramin, and Scott Foundas. "'47 Ronin': The Inside Story of Universal's Samurai Disaster." *Variety*, December 30, 2013. https://variety.com/2013/film/news/47-ronin-box-office-bomb-1201012170.

Statista Research Department. "Global Cinema Advertising Expenditure 2014–2021." Statista, March 7, 2022. https://www.statista.com/statistics/273715/global-cinema-advertising-expenditure.

## CHAPTER 4

ATD Research. *2019 State of the Industry*. American Management Association, December 2019. https://www.td.org/research-reports/2019-state-of-the-industry.

Barshay, Jill. "Proof Points: Later School Start Time Gave Small Boost to Grades but Big Boost to Sleep, New Study Finds." The Hechinger Report, April 26, 2021. https://hechingerreport.org/proof-points-later-school-start-time-gave-small-boost-to-grades-but-big-boost-to-sleep-new-study-finds.

Brinkerhoff, R. O. "The Success Case Method: A Strategic Evaluation Approach to Increasing the Value and Effect of Training." *Advances in Developing Human Resources* 7, no. 1 (2005), 86–101. https://doi.org/10.1177/1523422304272172

Deming, W. Edwards. *Out of the Crisis, reissue.* Boston: MIT Press, 2018.

Dorrow, Laura G., and Mary E. Boyle. "Instructor Feedback for College Writing Assignments in Introductory Classes." *Journal of Behavioral Education* 8, no. 1 (1998): 115–129. https://doi.org/10.1023/A:1022820925481.

Duckworth, Angela Lee, Teri A. Kirby, Eli Tsukayama, Heather Berstein, and K. Anders Ericsson. "Deliberate Practice Spells Success: Why Gritter Competitors Triumph at the National Spelling Bee." *Social Psychological and Personality Science* 2, no. 2 (2011): 174–181. https://doi.org/10.1177/1948550610385872.

Duncan, Greg J., Chantelle J. Dowsett, Amy Claessens, Katherine Magnuson, Aletha C. Huston, Pamela Klebanov, Linda S. Pagani, et al. "School Readiness and Later Achievement." *Developmental Psychology* 43, no. 6 (2007): 1428–1446. https://doi.org/10.1037/0012-1649.43.6.1428.

Freifeld, Lorri. "2017 Training Industry Report." *Training*, November 9, 2017. https://trainingmag.com/trgmag-article/2017-training-industry-report.

Hillaker, Harry. "Tribute to John R. Boyd." Code One, Lockheed Martin Aeronautics Company, July 1997.

Hinshaw, Ada Sue, Carolyn H. Smeltzer, and Jan R. Atwood "Innovative Retention Strategies for Nursing Staff." *The Journal of Nursing Administration* 17, no. 6 (1987): 8–16. PMID: 3647116.

Holton, Elwood F., and Timothy Baldwin. "Making Transfer Happen: An Action Perspective on Learning Transfer Systems." *Advances in Developing Human Resources* 8, no. 4 (2000): 1–6.

Holtzapple, Carol, Suzy Griswold, Noreen Nouza, and Cami Berry. "Effectiveness of the Capturing Kids' Hearts Process: Resarch Summary of the 2008–2009 Randomized Controlled Trial." Flippen Education Research, 2016. https://flippengroup.com/downloads/CKH-2008-2009Randomized-Controlled-Trial-Research-Summary.pdf

Johnson, David W. Roger T. Johnson. "Learning Together and Alone: Overview and Meta-analysis." *Asia Pacific Journal of Education* 22, no. 1 (2006): 95–105. https://doi.org/10.1080/0218879020220110.

Kluger, Avraham N., and Angelo DeNisi. "The Effects of Feedback Interventions on Performance: A Historical Review, A Meta-Analysis, and a Preliminary Feedback Intervention Theory." *Psychological Bulletin* 119, no. 2 (1996): 254–284. https://doi.org/10.1037/0033-2909.119.2.254.

Krane, Vikki. "The Mental Readiness Form as a Measure of Competitive State Anxiety." *The Sport Psychologist* 8, no. 2 (1994): 189–202. https://doi.org/10.1123/tsp.8.2.189.

Kupritz, Virginia. "The Relative Impact of Workplace Design on Training Transfer." *Human Resource Development Quarterly* 13, no. 4 (2002): 427–447. https://doi.org/10.1002/hrdq.1042.

Ma, Xingjun, Sudanthi Wijewickrema, Yun Zhou, Shuo Zhou, Stephen O'Leary, and James Bailey. "Providing Effective Real-Time Feedback in Simulation-Based Surgical Training." In *Medical Image Computing and Computer-Assisted Intervention—MICCAI 2017*, edited by M. Descoteau, L. Maier-Hein, A. Franz, P. Jannin, D. Collins, and S. Duchesne, 566–574. New York: Springer, 2017. https://doi.org/10.1007/978-3-319-66185-8_64.

National Research Council. *Review and Assessment of the Health and Productivity Benefits of Green Schools: An Interim Report*. Washington, DC: The National Academies Press, 2006. https://doi.org/10.17226/11574.

Nowack, Kenneth, and Paul J. Zak. *Sustain High Performance with Psychological Safety (TD at Work Guide)*. ATD Press, 2021.

Recardo, Ronald J. "Conducting a Readiness Assessment: A Foundation for Solid Teamwork." *National Productivity Review* 18, no. 2(2012): 29–34. https://doi.org/10.1002/npr.4040180206.

Schrader, Jessica. "Countries with the Best Public School Systems." Metro Parent, April 1, 2018. https://www.metroparent.com/education/school-issues/countries-with-the-best-public-school-systems.

Staron, Lidia. "Employee Training and Development: How to Measure the ROI of Training Programs." HR Toolbox, updated December 16, 2021. https://www.toolbox.com/hr/learning-development/articles/employee-training-and-development-how-to-measure-the-roi-of-training-programs.

Tett, Robert P., and John P. Meyer. "Job Satisfaction, Organizational Commitment, Turnover Intention, and Turnover: Path Analyses Based on Meta-analytic Findings." *Personnel Psychology* 46, no. 2 (1993): 259–293. https://doi.org/10.1111/j.1744-6570.1993.tb00874.x.

Vowels, Christopher, and Steven Aude. "The Psychological Intangibles of Soldier Readiness." *NCO Journal* (November 2019): 1–21. https://www.armyupress.army.mil/Portals/7/nco-journal/images/2019/November/Intangibles-1/Measuring-Intangibles.pdf.

## CHAPTER 7

"General Election: Trump vs. Clinton." Real Clear Politics, accessed May 23, 2022. https://www.realclearpolitics.com/epolls/2016/president/us/general_election_trump_vs_clinton-5491.html.

Alexander, Veronika, Collin Blinder, and Paul J. Zak. "Why Trust an Algorithm? Performance, Cognition, and Neurophysiology." *Computers in Human Behavior* 89 (July 2018): 279–288. https://doi.org/10.1016/j.chb.2018.07.026.

*B2B Lead Generation and Client Acquisition Trends Report*. LinkedSelling, accessed June 17, 2022. https://linkedselling.com/wp-content/uploads/2021/06/B2B-Lead-Gen-Client-Acq-Trends-Report-Public-PDF-2021.pdf

Baker, Sherry, and David L. Martinson. "The TARES Test: Five Principles for Ethical Persuasion." *Journal of Mass Media Ethics* 16, nos. 2–3 (2011): 148–175. https://doi.org/10.1080/08900523.2001.9679610.

Berke, Jeremy. "Here's How Much it Costs for a University to Host a Presidential Debate." *Business Insider*, October 9, 2016. https://www.businessinsider.com/how-much-it-costs-to-host-a-presidential-debate-2016-10.

Bryant, Gregory A., and Martie G. Haselton. "Vocal Cues of Ovulation in Human Females." *Biology Letters* 5, no. 1 (2009): 12–15. https://doi.org/10.1098/rsbl.2008.0507.

Falk, Emily B., Elliot T. Berkman, Traci Mann, Brittany Harrison, and Matthew D. Lieberman. "Predicting Persuasion-Induced Behavior Change from the Brain." *Journal of Neuroscience* 30, no. 25 (June 2010): 8421–8424. https://doi.org/10.1523/JNEUROSCI.0063-10.2010.

Hirsh, Jacob. B., Sonia K. Kang, and Galen V. Bodenhausen. "Personalized Persuasion: Tailoring Persuasive Appeals to Recipients' Personality Traits." *Psychological Science* 23, no. 6 (2012): 578–581. https://doi.org/10.1177/0956797611436349.

Little, Anthony C., Benedict C. Jones, D. Michail Burt, and David I. Perrett. "Preferences for Symmetry in Faces Change Across the Menstrual Cycle." *Biological Psychology* 76, no. 3 (October 2007): 209–216. https://doi.org/10.1016/j.biopsycho.2007.08.003.

Matz, Sandra, M. Kosinski, Gideon Nave, and David Stillwell. "Psychological Targeting as an Effective Approach to Digital Mass Persuasion." *Proceedings of the National Academy of Sciences* 114, no. 48 (November 2017): 12714–12719. https://doi.org/10.1073/pnas.1710966114.

Merolla, Jennifer L., Guy Burnett, Kenneth V. Pyle, Sheila Ahmadi, and Paul J. Zak. "Oxytocin and the Biological Basis for Interpersonal and Political Trust." *Political Behavior* 35, no. 4 (2013): 753–776. https://doi.org/10.1007/s11109-012-9219-8.

Miller, Geoffrey, Joshua M. Tybur, and Brent D. Jordan. "Ovulatory Cycle Effects on Tip Earnings by Lap Dancers: Economic Evidence for Human Estrus?" *Evolution and Human Behavior* 28, no. 6 (November 2007): 375–381. https://doi.org/0.1016/j.evolhumbehav.2007.06.002.

Morris, Brandi S., Polymeros Chrysochou, Jacob Dalgaard Christensen, Jacob L. Orquin, Jorge Barraza, Paul J. Zak, and Panagiotis Mitkidis. "Stories vs. Facts: Triggering Emotion and Action-taking on Climate Change." *Climatic Change* 154, no. 2 (May 2019): 19–36. https://doi.org/10.1007/s10594-019-02425-6.

Pew Research Center. "An Examination of the 2016 Electorate, Based on Validated Voters." August 9, 2018. https://www.pewresearch.org/politics/2018/08/09/an-examination-of-the-2016-electorate-based-on-validated-voters.

Porges, Eric C., Karen E. Smith, and Jean Decety. "Individual Differences in Vagal Regulation Are Related to Testosterone Responses to Observed Violence." *Frontiers in Psychology* 6, no. 19 (February 2015). https://doi.org/10.3389/fpsyg.2015.00019.

Thaler, Richard, and Cass Sunstein. "Libertarian Paternalism." *The American Economic Review* 93, no. 2 (2003): 175–79. https://doi.org/10.1257/000282803321947001.

Zak, Paul J., Robert Kurzban, Sheila Ahmadi, Ronal S. Swerdloff, Jang Park, Levan Efremidze, Karen Redwine, Karla Morgan, and William Matzner. "Testosterone Administration Decreases Generosity in the Ultimatum Game." *PLoS One* 4, no. 12 (2009): e8330. https://doi.org/10.1037/journal.pone.0008330.

Zoltners, Andris A., P. K. Sinha, Sally E. Lorimer, Tania Lennon, and Emily Alexander. "Why Women Are the Future of B2B Sales." *Harvard Business Review*, May 2020. https://hbr.org/2020/05/why-women-are-the-future-of-b2b-sales.

## CHAPTER 8

Danzinger, Pamela. "The $242 Billion Business of Corporate Gifting Pivoted from a Routing to a Priority in the Pandemic." *Forbes*, September 1, 2021. https://www.forbes.com/sites/pamdanziger/2021/09/01/the-242-billion-business-of-corporate-gifting-turned-from-a-routine-to-a-priority-in-the-pandemic/?sh=399fc1206ac2.

Franklin, Benjamin. "The Deformed and Handsome Leg." American Philosophical Society. Pierpont Morgan Library, incomplete (draft). Before November 23, 1780. https://founders.archives.gov/documents/Franklin/01-34-02-0021.

Gottman, John Mordechai, and Robert Wayne Levenson. "The Timing of Divorce: Predicting When a Couple Will Divorce over a 14-Year Period." *Journal of Marriage and Family* 62, no. 3 (2000): 737–745. https://doi.org/10.1111/j.1741-3737.2000.00737.x.

Guenzi, Paolo. "How Ritual Delivers Performance." *Harvard Business Review*, February 25, 2013. https://hbr.org/2013/02/how-ritual-delivers-performanc.

Hamermesh, Daniel S. "Life Satisfaction, Loneliness and Togetherness, with an Application to Covid-19 Lock-Downs." *Review of Economics of the Household* 18, no. 4 (2020): 983–1000. https://doi.org/10.1007/s11150-020-09495-x.

Hecht, Anna. "Here's How Much Americans Spend on Dating at Every Age." CNBC online, February 18, 2020. https://www.cnbc.com/2020/02/18/how-much-americans-spend-on-dating-at-every-age.html.

Johnson, Craig. "New Study: The #1 Supermarket for Customer Satisfaction." Clark.com, April 7, 2022. https://clark.com/shopping-retail/best-grocery-stores-customer-satisfaction.

Kotler, Steven. *The Art of the Impossible: A Peak Performance Primer*. New York: Harper Wave, 2021.

Liddell, Christine, Chris Morris, Harriet Thomson, and Ciara Guiney. "Excess Winter Deaths in 30 European Countries 1980–2013: A Critical Review of Methods." *Journal of Public Health* 38, no. 4 (2016): 806–814. https://doi.org/10.1093/pubmed/fdv184.

"Online Dating." Statista, updated December 2021. https://www.statista.com/outlook/dmo/eservices/dating-services/online-dating/worldwide.

Penenberg, Adam L. "Social Networking Affects Brains like Falling in Love." *Fast Company*, July 1, 2010. https://www.fastcompany.com/1659062/social-networking-affects-brains-falling-love.

Peterson, Chrisopher, Nansook Park, Nicholas Hall, and Martin E.P. Seligman. "Zest and Work." *Journal of Organizational Behavior* 30, no. 2 (2009): 161–172. https://doi.org/10.1002/job.584.

Stavrova, Olga. "Having a Happy Spouse is Associated with Lowered Risk of Mortality." *Psychological science* 30, no. 5 (May 2019): 798–803. https://doi.org/10.1177/0956797619835147.

Tergesen, Anne, and Miho Inada. "It's Not a Stuffed Animal, It's a $6,000 Medical Device." *Wall Street Journal*, June 21, 2010. https://www.wsj.com/articles/SB10001424052748704463504575301051844937276.

Terris, Elizabeth T., Laura E. Beavin, Jorge A. Barraza, Jeff Schloss, and Paul J. Zak. "Endogenous Oxytocin Release Eliminates In-Group Bias in Monetary Transfers with Perspective-Taking." *Frontiers in Behavioral Neuroscience* 12, no. 35 (2018). https://doi.org/10.3389/fnbeh.2018.0035.

Vuleta, Branka. "Divorce Rate in America [35 Stunning Stats for 2022]." Legal Jobs, January 28, 2021. https://legaljobs.io/blog/divorce-rate-in-america.

Made in the USA
Las Vegas, NV
05 May 2023